THEATRE LIBRARY ASSOCIATION

The Theatre Library Association is a non-profit organization established in 1937 to advance the interests of all those involved in collecting and preserving theatrical materials and in utilizing those materials for purposes of scholarship. The membership is international and includes public and private institutions as well as librarians, curators, private collectors, historians, professors, theatre designers, actors, writers, and all other interested persons.

The Theatre Library Association meets annually to conduct its business in the fall of each year. It presents a day of conferences and programs during the annual meeting of the American Library Association, usually in late spring or early summer.

It publishes Broadside, *a quarterly newsletter,* Performing Arts Resources, *an annual journal, and occasional conference compendia.*

It is governed by a constitution which provides for a board of directors elected by the membership and officers elected by the board.

THE THEATRE LIBRARY ASSOCIATION BOOK AWARDS

Two awards are presented annually for books of unusual merit and distinction in the fields served by the Association.

The George Freedley Award, *established in 1968, honors work in the field of theatre published in the United States. Only books with subjects related to live performance will be considered. They may be biography, history or criticism.*

The Theatre Library Association Award, *established in 1973, honors a book published in the United States in the field of recorded performance, which includes motion pictures, radio and television.*

Works ineligible for both awards are textbooks; anthologies; collections of essays previously published in other sources; reprints; works on dance, ballet and opera; plays and similar dramatic works. Translations of significant works, other than play texts, will be considered. Entries will be judged on the basis of scholarship, readability and general contribution of knowledge to the fields served by the Association. No galley sheets or proofs will be accepted. Books nominated for awards must be published in the calendar year prior to the presentation of the awards and must be received no later than March 1 of the year following publication.

Nominations are to be submitted in writing to the Chair, Book Awards Committee, in care of the Theatre Library Association, 111 Amsterdam Avenue, New York, N.Y. 10023.

PERFORMING ARTS RESOURCES, *the annual publication of the Theatre Library Association, is designed to gather and disseminate scholarly articles dealing with the location of resource materials relating to theatre, film, television and radio; descriptions, listings, or evaluations of the contents of such collections, whether public or private; and monographs of previously unpublished original source material.*

All manuscripts to be submitted must be typed cleanly, on one side only, double-spaced and adhering to the style and method described in the MLA Style Sheet, Second Edition. *Photographs and other illustrations will be used at the discretion of the editors.*

Please submit manuscripts with covering letter and return postage to:

Performing Arts Resources
c/o B.N. Cohen-Stratyner
265 Riverside Drive
New York, New York 10025

PERFORMING ARTS RESOURCES

Edited by Ginnine Cocuzza
and
Barbara Naomi Cohen-Stratyner

VOLUME ELEVEN

SCENES AND MACHINES FROM THE 18TH CENTURY:

The Stagecraft of Jacopo Fabris and Cityoen Boullet

translated by C. Thomas Ault
edited by Barbara Cohen-Stratyner

Published by the Theatre Library Association

The Library of Congress catalogued this serial as follows:
Performing Arts Resources
    Vols. for 1974—issued by the Theatre Library Association
    ISSN 0360-3814
1. Performing arts—Library resources—United States—Periodicals
I. Theatre Library Association
Z6935.P46   016.7902'08   75-646287
ISBN 0-932610-08-0

Designed by Barbara Stratyner
Produced by BookCrafters, Inc., Chelsea, Michigan
Manufactured in the United States of America

TABLE OF CONTENTS

Instruction in Theatre Architecture reproduced with the kind permission of the Department of Manuscripts, Royal Library of Denmark, Copenhagen.

Fabris Drawings reproduced with the kind permission of the Department of Prints and Drawings, The Royal Museum of Fine Arts, Copenhagen.

Boullet *Essay* reproduced with the kind permission of the Theatremuseum, Munich, Federal Republic of Germany.

FROM THE EDITORS

The Theatre Library Association is pleased to add *Scenes and Machines from the Eighteenth Century* to the growing list of *Performing Arts Resources*. C. Thomas Ault's translations of technical manuals by Jacopo Fabris (1760) and Cityoen Boullet (1801) are invaluable sources for scholars and designers interested in the structural basis of Baroque theatrical architecture.

Both Fabris' *Instruction in Theatre Architecture and Mechanics* and Boullet's *Essay on the Art of Constructing Theatres, Their Machines and Their Operations* can teach a contemporary reader to design a stage, rig a flying machine or even create a system in perspective drafting for renderings or scene painting. Each book will also provide scholars with fascinating information on the theatrical milieu at the turn of the 19th century. Fabris' *Instruction* and an appended collection of drawings teach the Italian style as imported to the Danish court. Boullet, writing in post-Revolutionary France, lectures his fellow citizens on fire prevention, landmark preservation and the importance of large orchestra pits, rehearsal rooms and sufficient wing space for the backstage artists. His *Essay*, serves as a most valuable source for scholars in opera, dance and music, as well as social history.

C. Thomas Ault is both a performance historian and a theatrical designer. An Assistant Professor of Theatre at Centenary College of Louisiana, he is, at the time of publication, in India on a Council for International Exchange of Scholars (Smithsonian Institution) Grant to study Rajasthani Folk Drama. His dissertation on Stage Machinery at the Paris Opera: 1770-1873 (The University of Michigan, 1983) and many articles on Baroque theatre design in Italy, Germany and France, have been highly praised.

For permission to reprint illustrations and to publish Ault's translations, the Editors of the Theatre Library Association thank the curatorial staffs and Directors of the following institutions:

  for Fabris' *Instruction,* the Department of Manuscripts, Royal Library of Denmark, in Copenhagen;

  for Fabris' drawings, the Department of Prints and Drawings, The Royal Museum of Fine Arts, Copenhagen; and

  for Boullet's *Essay,* the Theatremuseum, Munich, the Federal Republic of Germany.

We are grateful that Volume Eleven of *Performing Arts Resources* is once more an opportunity for international cooperation in the continuing process of providing translations of valuable source materials for theatre scholars.

Performing Arts Resources will continue to make available reference material to augment library collections and to give researchers access to rare material. We will publish conference papers, articles and essays that will enable librarians, archivists and scholars to locate, identify and classify information on theatre, film, broadcasting and popular entertainment. Future projects include volumes on annotated bibliographies of plays, dance and the full range of source material in popular entertainments. The Theatre Library Association is also planning publication of a Style Manual for scholars, students, writers and curators in the Performing and Broadcast Arts. We welcome our readers' comments and suggestions.

Ginnine Cocuzza
Barbara Naomi Cohen-Stratyner

ACKNOWLEDGEMENTS

Of the many people and institutions who have contributed to this book I am particularly indebted to The Royal Library and the Royal Museum of Fine Arts, Copenhagen, for having provided me with the manuscript and drawings by Jacopo Fabris used in this work, and the Theatermuseum, Munich, for providing their copy of Cityoen Boullet's *Essay* from which the present translation as well as the plates were taken. I am also grateful to the Theatre Department of The University of Michigan for funds and facilities used to complete the final editing of Boullet's *Essay.* A special thanks is owed to Dr. Barbara Cohen-Stratyner and the Theatre Library Association for choosing this work to be Volume Eleven of *Performing Arts Resources* and to Margaret Knapp for her enthusiastic response to the Boullet manuscript and her referral to TLA for publication.

I am extremely indebted to June Hager for her superb primary translation of Jacopo Fabris' *Instruction* and to Dr. Orville Kurth Larson for reading my primary translation of Boullet's *Essay* and making many valuable suggestions which helped bring it to its final form. Finally, I am grateful to my family for having tolerated me during the final days of preparing the manuscript for this work.

INTRODUCTION

by C. Thomas Ault

The eighteenth century was a time of consolidation and sophistication of the stage techniques developed in the extremely innovative century preceding it. The works of Jacopo Fabris and Cityoen Boullet form opposite ends of the spectrum embracing the changes which took place as a part of the process.

It is hard to overestimate the value of these works to the history of stage design and stagecraft. Sources of any kind on stage design previous to the twentieth century are rare; works such as these, with detailed descriptions and instructions for the design, construction and operation of stages and their machines are rare enough to be called extraordinary. Fabris is the sole eighteenth century representative of the Italian system of stagecraft so far brought to light. Boullet is equally important since his work covers the French system of stagecraft. Although there are other extant works on the French system, none are so complete in their details and descriptions as Boullet.

Not much is known about either Fabris or Boullet. Fabris was primarily a scene painter although he not only painted but built stages for some distinguished patrons of the arts, including Frederick the Great of Prussia and Frederick V of Denmark. Even less is known about Boullet but the salient fact that he was the Head Machinist at the Théâtre des Arts (The Paris Opera) in 1801 is enough to establish him as one of the leading authorities on the French system.

Jacopo Fabris' apparently checkered career is filled with hiatuses. He was born in Venice in 1689 but does not emerge as an artist until 1719 when he appeared as a court painter for the Margrave Karl-Wilhelm von Baden-Durlach at Karlsruhe where he also painted scenery. He left the Margrave in 1721 but, in 1724, began two years as a scene painter at the Hamburg Opera under art patron Graf Ahlefeldt. He must have been very busy there, for in that period the enthusiastic Graf produced twenty-five new works of all kinds, including classical works, pastorals, folk works, comedies, intermezzi, etc. Such a wide repertory must have broadened Fabris' experience greatly.

Fabris apparently remained in Hamburg until c.1730 when he vanished for another ten years. He re-emerged in 1742 at the prestigious court of Europe's leading drill master and patron of the arts, Frederick the Great of Prussia.

Exactly what he did at Frederick's new center of art and culture in Berlin is not entirely clear. He writes that he built a small "Teatrum" (sic) at court and a larger one in the town. If by this he meant he was the architect of any theatres for the Prussian monarch, his statement is contrary to the known facts, for Georg Wenzeslaus von Knobelsdorff was Frederick's court architect at this time and is well known for having built the Berlin Opera House.

However, there is an explanation for this statement other than the immediate impression that Fabris may have sought to inflate his reputation through resumé enhancement. He probably was using the word "Teatrum" (i.e., *Theatrum)* only to refer to the stage. Such usage was not uncommon during Fabris' time. This being the case, Fabris then worked under Knobelsdorff as the designer and builder of the stages and machines for these theatres in Berlin. The designs in his works presented here certainly attest to his competence to have done such work. Also, he mentions the work he did on the "large stage" in Berlin in Folio V.

Fabris moved for the last time in 1746 when he left the Prussian court in Berlin to settle at the Royal Court of Denmark. Theatre was in its infancy when he arrived in Copenhagen. The previous king, Christian VI, had had little use for it, but his son, Frederick V, who ascended to the throne in the year of Fabris' arrival, was of the same spirit as his more famous Prussian neighbor, Frederick the Great. Under Frederick V, theatre found an enthusiastic patron who was to found a truly national Theatre with works in Danish as well as French and Italian as was the vogue in Europe at that time. Fabris was very active in this "New Berlin" where he had the opportunity to participate in the creation of a new Theatre for Denmark.

In Copenhagen, he said that he built two theatres for the Danish comedians (i.e., players), and one "where the operas are performed." Again one must be cautious in the interpretation of his use of the word, "Teatern." He did build and equip a stage in the Charlottenborg court where Italian operas were performed. He served in the same capacity to the court architect, Nicolai Eigtved, as he had for Knobelsdorff in Berlin, but there was only one theatre, not two. It was built at Kongens Nytorv and Fabris built and equipped the stage for its opening in 1748.

The following year Fabris painted new sets for *Allesandro nell' Indie,* (Alexander in India), text by Pietro Metastasio, to be used by the operatic troupe in this new theatre. Three sketches by Fabris of scenes from that opera, in his collected drawings at the Royal Museum of Fine Arts, are presented here.

Having finished the stage at Kongens Nytorv and the new operatic scenery to be used on it, Jacopo Fabris' career in Theatre came to an end. Always active as a perspective painter, he apparently spent a number of years as a teacher of this art before he died in his quarters at Charlottenborg, December 16, 1761.

His work, *Instruction in Theatre Architecture and Mechanics,* given here in English for the first time, is volume four of a five volume work entitled, *Geometrisch-Perspectivisch Architectischen Lectionen,* Copenhagen, 1760. The manuscript is preserved at The Royal Library in Copenhagen, Tottsche Collection, Folio number 295. Book Four was first published in 1930 by Torbin Krogh in the original German under the title, *Jacopo Fabris Instruction in der Teatralischen Architectur und Mechanique, Udgivet og Forsynet Med Inledning af Torben Krogh,* Copenhagen. Krogh's commentaries on Fabris' life and work are excellent.

Fabris obviously was not an illustrious artist. Neither does he appear to have been much of an innovator. However, his work at two royal courts as designer and builder of stages and stage machinery certainly recommends him highly as a theatre technician and practical man of the stage. To have been a scene painter in these courts as well as others reflects highly on his competence as a master artist of his day.

Consequently, the work he left behind is of inestimable value as a reflection of the general practices of this time, not just those of one person. Comparison of his work to earlier documents of the seventeenth century shows that he continued to work in traditional modes using basic concepts and methods that had been worked out before he was even born.[1]

His instructions for painting perspective scenery are unique for their practicality, clarity and completeness of detail yet similar if not identical methods had undoubtedly been used by earlier painters. His theatre designs and ground plans are typical of seventeenth century stage design. The empty *prospetta*[2] (prospect) behind the scenic area of the stage for the wings and borders, the long slots in the stage floor for the shutters which closed the scenes before back drops came into common use and angled wings shown on his ground plan for a theatre in the collection at The Royal Museum of Fine Arts, (Plate I), are all typical of seventeenth century Italian designs.[3]

Fabris was one of the last practitioners of the older Italian system of stagecraft and stage design. Yet, there are also some new elements in his work, particularly in his designs for flying machines. His design in Plate V (The Royal Museum of Fine Arts) shows a cross section of a completely equipped stage, including a fully rigged horizontal flying machine with a machinist operating it. The machinist has a rope in his hands which he is using to control the descent of the counterweight which powers the towing line. This drawing is the first to show this rope called a regulator. The whole rigging of the counterweight portion of the machine, including the regulator, is the type which was to become standard for just about every machine in the later French system. This drawing is an important technical bridge between the old Italian and the new French system.

A curious element in Fabris' ground plans is a symbol which appears to represent a cyclorama. Is it a cyclorama? If so, then the cyclorama appeared much earlier than is commonly thought. If it is not a cyclorama, what is it?

Fabris' division of his *Instruction* into twenty "Folios" falls into two parts. The first ten folios cover the design of the stage and its machines. The second part deals with theatre building, scene painting and designs for various types of sets commonly used on the stage during his time. The collection from The Royal Museum of Fine Arts, numbered as Plates I through XII, is eclectic and some of the drawings may have been intended for another work on stage design. Fabris' gentle style of writing is that of an older man passing the torch to the next generation whom he addresses as "Dear reader." His work is not only informative but a pleasure to read.

. . . . .

Even less is known about Boullet than Fabris. He signed his work *Essay on the Art of Constructing Theatres, their Machines and their Operations,* Paris, 1801 simply as "Cityoen Boullet," (Citizen Boullet), in the fashion of the French revolution, so not even his full name is known. What he does say about himself, however, is impressive enough to establish him as probably having been the leading authority of his time on stagecraft and stage design in France.

Boullet must have had at least forty years experience behind him when his *Essay* appeared in Germinal, An 9 (April, 1801). He stated that he learned his craft from Arnoult, whom he calls his master. Arnoult, (also spelled Arnould and Arnout) was *Machiniste du Roi,* or "The King's Machinist," from 1747 till c.1757 when his name became obscured by Girault (also spelled Giraud). Giraud co-authored the section, "Machines du Théâtre" in *L'Encyclopédie* by Diderot and D'Alambert, (Paris, 1765-1772). Boullet very likely worked with Girault too, since the latter was an "Architect of Fine Pleasures and Machinist of the Paris Opera" when he wrote for Diderot and D'Alambert.

Apparently Boullet also worked with the famous Italian, Niccolo Servandoni (also spelled Servadoni), who was the last of the great Italians to work as a chief machinist in Paris.[4] In fact, he may have been the major architect of the French system of stage machines as Boullet made this revealing comment about him:

> Servadoni never would have imagined that the techniques
> and operations designed by his hardy hand would languish,
> nor would one of his genius. . . . .

Was it indeed Servadoni's "hardy hand" that designed the new style of machines and techniques destined to become known as "The

French System?"[5] If so, then Boullet worked with the creator of the very system he describes so well in his work.

Boullet's work is so thorough that it is difficult to compare it to other works which cover the French system. The earliest work, "Machines du Theatre" by Girault and Radel in *L'Encyclopédie* can only be fully appreciated through reference to Boullet's *Essay*. Though Girault and Radel provide many excellent drawings, their text often consists of little more than identifications of the labeled parts in the drawings. The same is true for C. Contant and J. Filippi's *Parallèle des principaux théâtres modernes de l'Europe . . . ,* Paris, 1860. Later works, J. Moynet's *L'Envers du téâtre,* Paris, 1873, and G. Moynet's *La machinerie téâtrale: trucs et decors,* Paris, 1893, provide interesting insights into the French system, well established by their times. However, their appeal is more to the connoisseur than to the expert or aspiring novice. Boullet wrote a text book from which one could rebuild the Paris Opera to specification if one so desired.

The first sixteen chapters treat the construction of the theatre, primarily the stage, and the design, construction and operation of the machines which are used on it. The last chapter is a summation of Boullet's views on Theatre which includes a description of how to mount an opera, using *Hecuba* as a model. This last chapter is extremely revealing as it demonstrates how a production was designed and mounted. It is the only known source for this procedure.

The remaining ten chapters (XVII-XXVI) treat the design and lighting of the auditorium, the foyers, rehearsal rooms, the orchestra pit, warehouse storage for the scenery, heating and fire prevention. They are as much an anecdotal history of the period as they are of Theatre. They are also charming as they reveal Boullet's own notions of what an evening in the Theatre ought to be for the audience, especially "the ladies" who, in his opinion, were indispensable for an operatic performance. Boullet supports his descriptions with thirteen excellent drawings at the end of the text.

Often strident, sometimes passionate, Boullet too wanted to pass the torch to the next generation but he wanted it to shine brightly for the glory of France. He cried for better theatres, especially theatres designed in collaboration with the experts who have to use them. His cry, old as it may be, is not unfamiliar, even today. Neither is his spirit; he wanted the very best and that is what he left in his *Essay* which is presented here in English to the general public for the first time.[6]

Footnotes

[1]Cf., MS. 3708, Biblioteca Palatina, Parma; MS. Majie, V. 4, pp. 1-38, Archivio di Stato, Parma; Fabrizio Carini Motta, *Costruzione de Teatri e Machine Teatrali,* (unpublished), Mantua, 1688: MS. Campori= .G .3 16, Biblioteca Estense, Modena.

[2]The *prospetta* is an empty area behind the sliding wings on the stage and behind the flying borders in the grid. Apparently it was used for special machines which were not stock equipment of the stage, such as apotheosis machines and machines for other special effects which were designed and built specifically for a particular production.

[3]Cf. The Tor di Nona Folio, Sir John Soane's Museum, London.

[4]Giovanni Nicolo Servandoni, (1695-1766), was a Florentine designer and follower of the Bibiena style of design. He introduced the *scena per angolo* to Paris and was noted for his "mute spectacles" at the Salle des Machines in the Tuileries. These "mute spectacles" were little more than grandiose displays of spectacular effects and changing scenery. Servandoni was active in Paris from circa 1728 till 1746 at the Paris Opera and intermittantly till 1758 at the Salle des Machines.

[5]C. Contant and J. Filippi identify three systems of stagecraft in their work, *Parallèle des principaux téâtres modernes de l'Europe . . . ,* Paris, 1860. These systems are the French, German and English.

[6]The same translation presented here previously appeared in *Design, Operation and Organization of Stage Machines at the Paris Opera: 1770-1873,* unpublished Ph.D. dissertation, The University of Michigan, 1983, by Cecil Thomas Ault Jr.

A NOTE ON THE TRANSLATIONS

There is a saying among translators that a translation is like a lover: the beautiful are not faithful and the faithful are not beautiful. I have tried to walk a fine line between these two extremes in order to create translations which are not only faithful to the original languages of their authors but graceful, if not always beautiful, in their rendering.

This was not a great problem with Fabris' work since I had the excellent assistance of June Hager whose keen sensitivity to language rendered a fine first translation which needed little revision beyond supplying technical terms and identifying problem areas in precise renderings of meanings of archaic stage terminology which have no modern equivalents in English. Also, Fabris' avuncular style of writing cannot help but be pleasing in any language.

Boullet's *Essay* is another matter entirely. Strident, sometimes passionate and always very technical, it bristles with esoteric stage vocabulary, much of which defies literal translation and most of which has no equivalents in modern English. Unlike Fabris' work, the problem was not simply one of supplying technical terms or identifying problem areas in precise renderings of meanings, but that of creating a whole vocabulary adequate to the task of rendering his work into good English.

Many dictionaries and other sources were consulted to find suitable words to create this vocabulary. However, frequently the only source for vocabulary was the work, itself, so the text was carefully compared to the drawings under discussion and suitable terms were created on the basis of form and function of the object in question. A few examples will illustrate the problems and some of the solutions adopted.

The term "wing" refers to an off stage area in modern stage terminology. However, a wing in the period of this work is piece of scenery and is known as a wing to everyone familiar with old stages. Thus, a wing had to remain a wing and the off stage areas (which acquired their modern names from the original use of the now empty space) were assigned no specific terms at all except "the off stage area to the right or left of the stage." In this case even a common English term would not do.

Sometimes the terms are direct translations from French sources which use terms more amenable to translation into English. The most frequently used of these sources was George Moynet's *La machinerie théâtrale, trucs et decors,* Paris, 1893. This is the last work to deal extensively with Boullet's type of stage and by this time French stage terminology had become more precise.

For example, both Boullet and Giraud *(L'Enclyclopédie)* use the term *faux chassis,* (i.e., "false frame" or "false wing") to refer to the frames mounted on the chariots to carry the wings on and off stage. The term makes perfectly good sense in French since a wing, also called a *chassis,* is the covered decoration (wing) seen by the audience and the uncovered, unseen frame *(faux chassis)* is false in the sense that it does not represent anything. However, the terms "false wing" or "false frame" are not only clumsy in English but utterly meaningless out of French context. Moynet's term, *mât,* is much simpler and to the point: it means "mast." Given the function of the *faux chassis* and the monosylabic clarity of "mast," it was preferred of the other alternatives.

Frequently, however, Boullet was the only source for stage terminology, particularly for terms referring to rigging. Direct translation of all his terms would have created a chaotic scramble of esoteric terms which, though charming, (as Theatre vocabulary is always charming in any language), would have inhibited understanding of the subject under discussion.

Thus, the drawings were consulted and *retrait a main,* (literally, "hand line") was translated as "regulator" since it is a rope used by a machinist to regulate the speed and movement of a machine in motion. Conversely, *retrait a contrepoid* remains literally, "counterweight line" since its literal translation is perfectly clear in its meaning; it is the rope from which the counterweight is suspended in a theatre machine.

As the Boullet work is the most comprehensive, it was used as the standard for all technical terms used in these translations, the only exceptions being terms used by Fabris which had no parallels in Boullet's work. Synonyms have been avoided for the sake of clarity. In places where precise renderings of meanings were difficult or terminology was a particular problem, footnotes have been provided with the original terms in French or German.

Instruction
in
Theatre, Architecture and
Mechanics

Book Four

In which will be found clear instructions for such things as how Theatre Buildings should be built and also designs for various arrangements such as the Auditorium, Stage, Machines, Movements, Flying Apparatus, and Steps which go up and down and must be arranged; also at the end there are Decors which are well suited for the purpose of instructing youth as it is desired that they be introduced (to the art).

by

Jacobo Fabris
Royal Danish Councilor

Copenhagen 1760

Instruction

in der

Teatralischen Architectur und Mechanique.

Viertes Buch

In welchen deütlich unterwiesen wird, wie solche Teatralische Gebäude sowoll gebauet, und auch dessen innwendige Einrichtung als, Amphiteatre, Teatre, Machinen, Bewegung, Flugwerck und Verzzen welche auf und niedergehn, eingerichtet werden müssen; auch habe am Ende etliche Decorationes die dazu erfoderlich sind, zum Unterricht der Jugend mit einbringen wollen.

von

Jacob Fabris

Königl. Dänischen Canzelley Rath.

Kopenhagen 1760.

FOLIO 1

The starting point, or that which must first be undertaken, is the proscenium-arch, or the opening of the stage. It should not be too wide, nor should it be too narrow. The correct proportion is twenty ells at the widest.[1] Here, however, I have given only eighteen ells. The height of the opening must be proportionately one third less than the width, once this latter dimension is ascertained. The decorations on each side must be simple and ornamental. There should be no great protuberances with colonnades, for these detract a great deal from the voice and result in the voice not being well enough heard. In order to show the opening in its entirety so that it can be thus constructed, I have also shown, in addition to the above, the orchestra *A* or the place where the musicians come to sit.

FOLIO 2

A great deal of space is needed for a stage, as I prove in this ground-plan, for all the scenery required for an opera must be set up on each side and there also must be enough room to change the scenes around, taking some away to set them up at another location.

The opening of the stage, or proscenium-arch *A* is eighteen ells wide, and three feet from this,[2] one begins to construct the first street. It must be one foot less on either side than is the proscenium-arch, measured from the center.[3] Here, I have made only four streets, as indicated by *1, 2, 3, 4*. However, one can construct as many as he likes. Nevertheless, I maintain that four will always be sufficient.

The area at the rear *B* must be deep and spacious, for here is where "distant views" will be represented. This area must have pillars set up on each side according to the arrangement *C* which can also serve to make a closed hall if one wants to hold mascarades on the stage. Thus, I have extended the streets up to the wall so that the chariots may be pushed far enough behind the pillars to close up the area.

The amphitheatre must be one foot wider on either side[4] and the distance from the proscenium-arch to the loge *D-E* must not be more than twenty ells, for it were more than that, one would not be able to hear the voices properly.

I have provided numerous apartments to the rear,[5] since many rooms are needed for various people to dress. There are also stairs at all places to enable one to go from above to the floor. Also, in such a building there must be many exits so that everyone can get out immediately in case of fire.

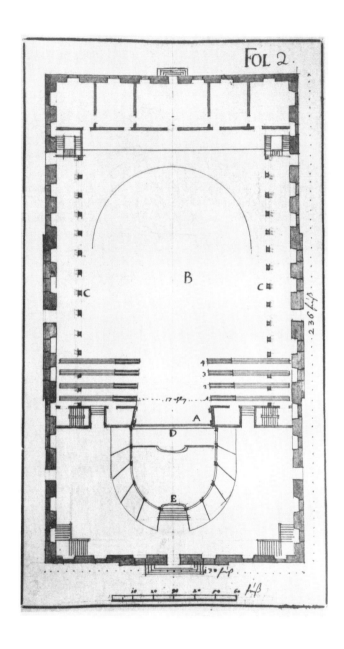

FOLIO 3

Here I have also made a longitudinal section in order to show the arrangement I made in the ground plan. The walls A must be high enough so that the borders can be raised out of sight and the space under the stage C must be deep enough so that the traps can be lowered sufficiently for persons appearing on them to remain hidden from view of the audience. For the stage floor D I have shown a rake or no more than two feet, starting at the back. I do not think this is excessive and it will be comfortable for walking.

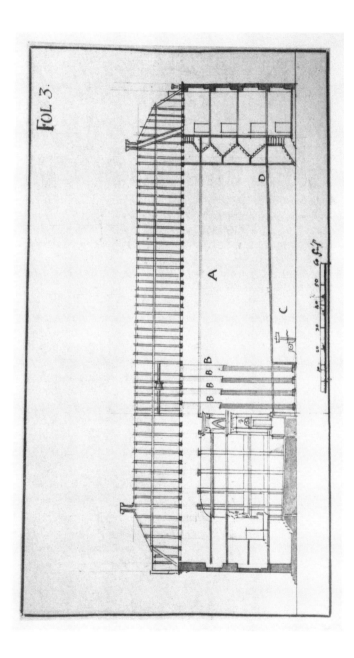

FOLIO 4

I have drawn this larger ground plan of the stage not only to make it more intelligible for myself, but also so that the dear reader may more clearly understand how such a stage should be constructed. The floor is laid out with joists which are not to be more than six inches wide. I have provided four sets, as seen by *1, 2, 3, 4,* and each set is provided with two chariots or "sliders." Between these is a street *A*[6] by which perspectives[7] may be slid onto the stage. For all of this, the perspective scale which I have provided in Folio 8 must be used. The first order (of wings)[8] must be placed seventeen feet from the center of the stage on each side. The second order must be placed seventeen feet from the center according to the second scale, the third order according to the third scale and the fourth order according to the fourth so that these orders will follow a diminished perspective.

The traps must not be too far from the proscenium arch because if someone must appear from below, he should be close enough to address the actor.[9] The horizontal axle with the drums mounted on it must be located at the rear to leave free space for moving between the chariots beneath the stage.[10] Also, there should not be any rigging in the way. I shall have more to say about this at an appropriate time.

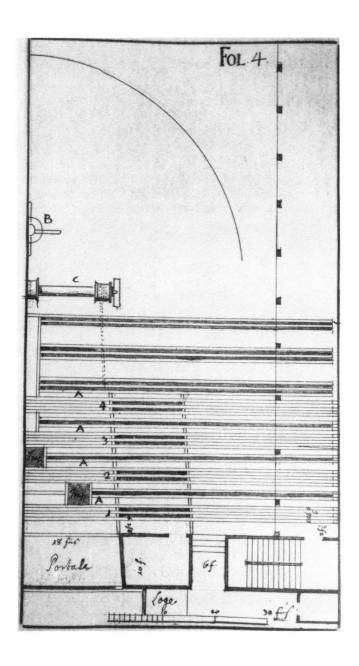

FOLIO 5

Three or four chariots may be set on a stage, as I have done in the large theatre in Berlin, with four chariots for each order as I show in this lesson. These orders are laid out from the center according to the perspective scales, as can be seen in this drawing.

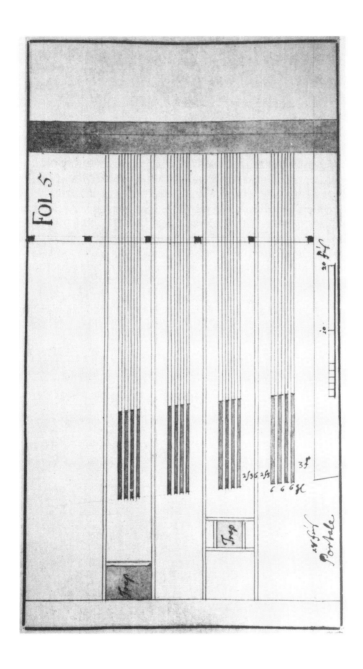

FOLIO 6

These are the chariots upon which the wings are firmly attached. They run on saddle-tracks *B* or in channel-tracks *A* and they run equally well on either type. The chariots *C* must be constructed like a ladder which one climbs, for instance, if it is necessary that something above be adjusted or perhaps to put up the lights or lamps to illuminate the stage. The four chariots in one order *B* move on saddle-tracks and could also run in channel-tracks. Likewise, the two chariots in order *A*, proving that one method will serve as well as the other.

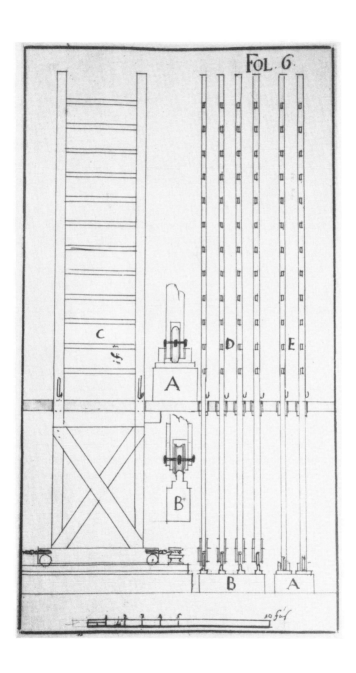

FOLIO 7

I mentioned above that two or four chariots can be put into one order. Thus, in this lesson I use four chariots whose functioning I shall now explain in detail.

There are four chariots, *1, 2, 3, 4,* in one order. Now, in order for these to move, there must be pulleys at the front and back, *A* and *B*,[11] through which the force to set the chariots in motion moves.[12] Thus, there must be at least three pulleys at the back and these must be large enough so that one can be set between the first and second chariot, another between the second and third, and another between the third and fourth chariots so as to be able pull and release all together.[13] The first and fourth chariots can be moved at the same time, or the second and fourth, or the first and third, however one likes, for when one is pulled forward the other moves back.

At the front, however, there must be at least double pulleys, one over the other as illustrated in *A*. The lines pass through these pulleys and around to the drum *B*. One line must pass around the drum above and the other below, since one pulls while the other releases.

The horizontal axle with the three drums must be set up in back as *C* in Folio 4 shows. Behind that is a standing windlass which draws up the rope from the center drum and causes the scenes to change. When this rope has accomplished a change of scenery, having played out above, it must be unfastened and then fastened below. Then it can be shifted back again. I hope I have made myself clear enough concerning moving and shifting.

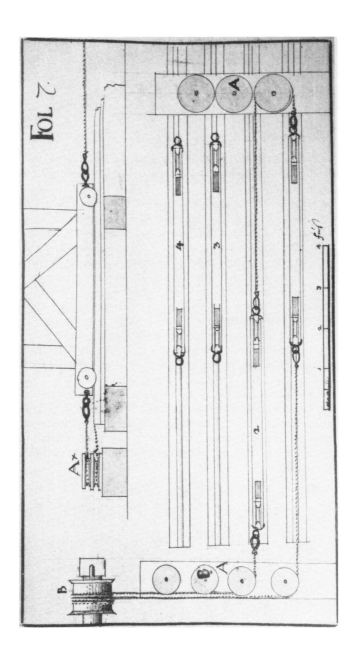

FOLIO 8

Sometimes a flying apparatus is required when a *Historie* is to be presented so I have desired to introduce the same here and show how it must be made.

The joists above the stage must be set three feet apart. Between two of them, *1* and *2,* a running track *X* will be made on the under side. The cart *A* will run on this track. Two long rollers *C* are exactly centered above the floor (of the stage). Drum *B* must stand on the floor (of the grid) and the ropes supporting the car *D* are wrapped around it. The ropes pass through the pulleys *E* in the cart *A* and carry the car from one side of the stage to the other.

A standing windlass *F* is necessary to move the machine from one side of the stage to the other. This windlass has a large drum *G* above, around which two strong ropes run on either side. These ropes, then, pass underneath by means of strong pulleys and run directly to the rings + of the cart *H,* pulling it from one side of the stage to the other.

This machine can also be set in motion by means of a weight, generally used for this purpose. However, I feel that the method just given is safer, for with the standing windlass, the machine can be held motionless at all times. One only has to make a mark on the rope *K* (and) when it reaches the drum it can be kept motionless as long as one desires.

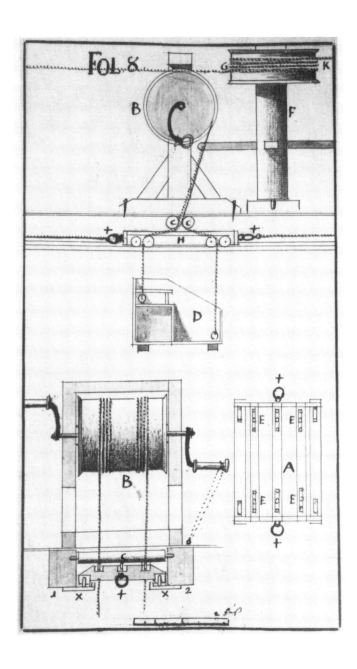

FOLIO 9

Sometimes traps are needed beneath the stage. These go up and down and let out ghosts or other things which must suddenly appear.

These machines, or traps *A*, are rectangular platforms which go up and down between four posts *1, 2, 3, 4,* and each post has pulleys *C* set into the center of the wood at the top. A windlass *D* is secured outside with two drums on either side, exactly centered on the posts, and here the ropes are securely fastened. These ropes go up over the pulleys *E*, come down and are made fast to the platform, so that when the windlass is turned, the platform can be both raised and lowered.

Trap *G* is oblong and trap *H* is square and both are constructed in the manner just described.

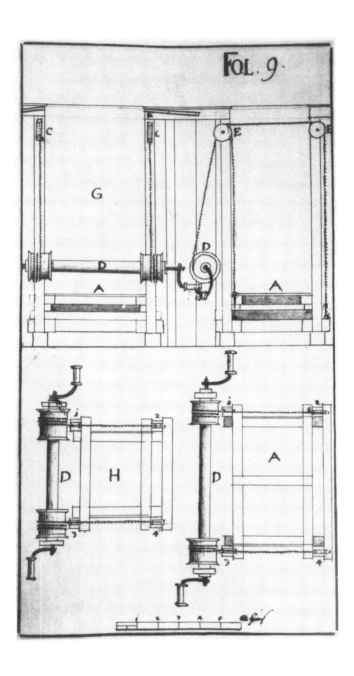

FOLIO 10

Here I show one half of a stage with its machines or wings numbered *1, 2, 3, 4, 5.* The first wing is twenty-four feet high and six feet wide. These wings must all be proportionate to each other according to the perspective scales, the first wing according to the ground scale,[14] the second according to the second perspective scale, the third according to the third (perspective scale) and the rest likewise to their scales so that all the heights and widths will conform to the perspective.

The ceilings of a room or chamber are also proportioned and drawn according to the scales, since these borders are also laid out from the center of the stage with these same scales so that everything will conform to the perspective according to the perspective scales. I also wished to present the proscenium arch *A* and the orchestra pit *B* in order to show the whole stage.

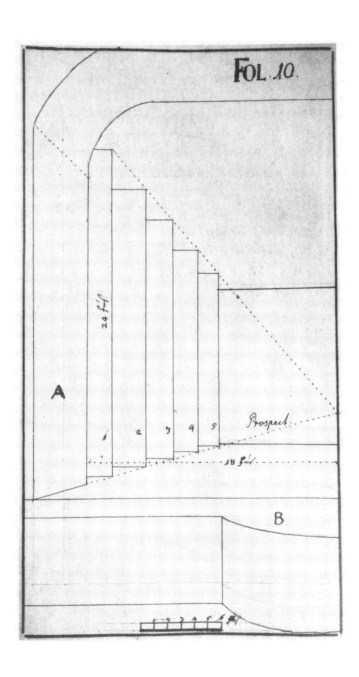

FOLIO 11

Whereas hitherto I have treated theatre architecture and mechanics, I thought it worthwhile to show a building of this kind. This is a facade or front elevation of an opera house and has the dimensions of the ground plan in Folio 2.

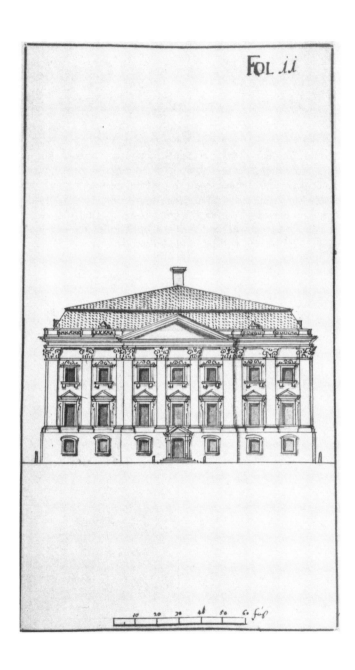

FOLIO 12

This building can also be a facade, depending on whether or not there is a sufficient vista to display it. Such a house must have many exits, so that in case of disaster all the spectators may get out at once. This house has eight exits, though not more than two are used. The others remain closed. However, they must be constructed so that they may be opened from the outside. Thus, should an incident occur, there be no delay and no one will be rendered hapless.

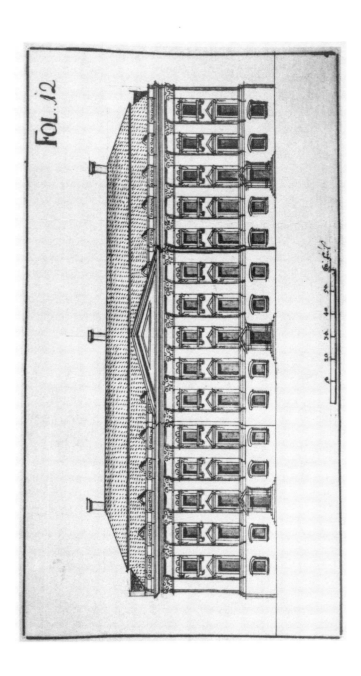

FOLIO 13

I promised to show everything required for a theatre so I think it is most necessary to instruct the dear reader on the scenes or decorations and how one should draw and paint these in perspective.

Drawing for the stage is quite different from other types of drawing. Hence, one must first draw up the ground scales[15] to provide the diminishing proportions of the perspective. To begin here, one must naturally use the ground foot[16] of which three feet in scale will be found in each scale. The next scale is one half inch less than the first, the third is one half inch less than the second and the fourth one half inch less than the third. All of these must be divided into twelve inches (per foot) proportionate to the perspective so that one can make twenty or thirty scales.

Then one takes a board which is two and a half feet long, as in B, and on this he marks out several inches on one side from top to bottom. Next, the board is placed on a large table and the square C is drawn. Eighteen inches are measured off (i.e. from the leading edge of the plank to the parallel side of the square) and the vanishing point D is set up from the lower or base line. From this point D, all the inches are drawn in perspective on the board B, and thus the eighteen inches represent the eighteen feet of the proscenium arch. After that, set your scenic piece or wing against the wall and mark out, top to bottom, as many feet as are marked out (i.e. on the board), 1, 2, 3, 4, 5, 6, 7, 8, 9, etc.

Then, set your board at the top of the wing, aligning number one on the board with number one on the wing, two with number two, and from the board draw the perspective lines as you see them drawn on the canvass F. The second wing must be proportioned with the second scale, the third with the third, the fourth with the fourth and so forth. To design perspective architecture one must likewise use the first scale with the first wing, the second scale with the second wing, the third with the third to design the perspective of theatrical wings as G illustrates.

When *distant views* are to be made a different board is used upon which perspective lines are drawn on both sides. Instead of placing the vanishing point eighteen inches away from the plank, use twice as many inches on each side and draw the perspective lines on board H. Then these must be drawn on the scenic pieces or wings. This is the easiest method for conveniently drawing everything on the wings, for the perspective runs from bottom to top and everything which is to be in conformity with the perspective is immediately at hand, drawn on the canvas and following the same perspective lines.

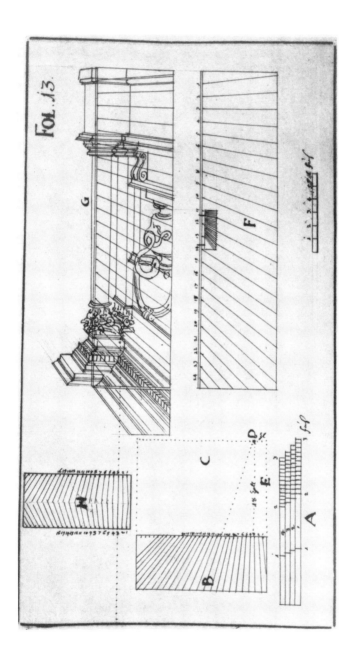

FOLIO 14

Henceforth some scenes which are generally needed in all operas will be presented. This is a vestibule or entrance in a royal palace and it can be made in many different ways. Each colonnade is a wing which must be drawn with the aid of the perspective board as was shown in the previous lesson.

FOLIO 15

Sometimes a chamber or room is also required for *Historie*. Therefore, I desired to present such a room here. It, likewise, can be made in many different ways.

FOLIO 16

An amphitheatre will also be necessary and can be made according to this one. Such an amphitheatre, likewise, can be represented in different ways and according to many methods.

FOLIO 17

I assume that a market place also will be needed occasionally. It too can be made in many different ways. This one here is only one representation of how it should be made.

FOLIO 18

When a *Historie* calls for it, a prison will sometimes be represented, so I show such a prison here to demonstrate how it should be
made. If necessary, it can be constructed in a different way.

FOLIO 19

Ruins will also be required sometimes and here I only suggest an idea for them. They can be made in many ways. However, it must be observed that the ruins must be depicted on every piece[17] and that everything is seen broadly and trivial details are not represented.

FOLIO 20

I close this fourth book with a large hall or temple. Thus I believe that I have explained myself and, to be sure, illustrated enough on theatre architecture and mechanics so that one may easily understand from my very clear explanations how each and every thing necessary for a theatre may be constructed. This is a special kind of work and very necessary these days since there are so many theatres in Europe.

End of Book Four

Footnotes

[1]According to the ground plan in Folio 2, eighteen ells are equal to forty feet. The Prussian elle was 0.6669 meters and the Austrian elle was 0.78 meters.

[2]By "three feet from this," Fabris means "three feet upstage of this."

[3]Fabris simply means that the first street is one foot further on stage than the edge of the proscenium arch.

[4]Fabris is measuring one foot from the edge of the proscenium arch on either side. Thus, the railings of the stalls, or boundaries of the orchestra are one foot wider than the proscenium arch on either side.

[5]The dressing rooms are built behind the up stage wall.

[6]The empty space in front of the orders or ranks of chariots are called streets. Technically, the entire empty space plus the slots for the chariots and shutters behind it are all considered part of the street.

[7]Note the shutter slots in each street to accommodate this operation.

[8]All the chariots on either side of the stage in one street are referred to collectively as an "order."

[9]This seems to presume that the actor will be located somewhere in the area of the deep proscenium arch, down stage of the scenery.

[10]This drawing shows the stage without any flooring to expose the parts beneath it. Therefore, the capstan *B* and all its attendant machinery are on the floor immediately beneath the stage.

[11]Fabris' labels are confusing here. The "front" or on stage pulleys are labeled twice with an *A* and a smudged *B*. The back pulleys are labeled *A*.

[12]The "force" is that applied by the rope which passes around these pulleys.

[13]The ropes must be detached and reset for each change of scenes. Thus, the pulley arrangement given here will accommodate any combination of rigging necessary to pull one chariot on stage while pulling another off.

[14]For "ground scale" Fabris uses the term "Land-Fuss" which means an actual foot measured on the ground in the first instance but diminishing up stage proportionately for each order of wings. See the scales in Folio 13.

[15]Here Fabris uses the term, "Fuss-Masstaben."

[16]Again, Fabris uses the term, "Land-Fuss."

[17]The text reads, ". . . nur wird observirt, dass auf jede Scene auch Ruinen kommen müssen . . . " He means to say that every scenic element, such as the wings, borders, back drops, etc., are painted.

A Collection of Drawings
by
Jacopo Fabris

Royal Museum of Fine Arts

Copenhagen

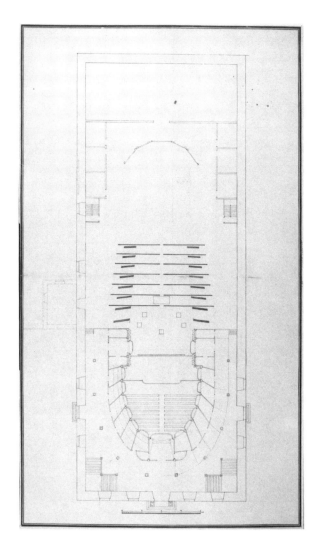

I. Ground Plan of a Theatre, undated

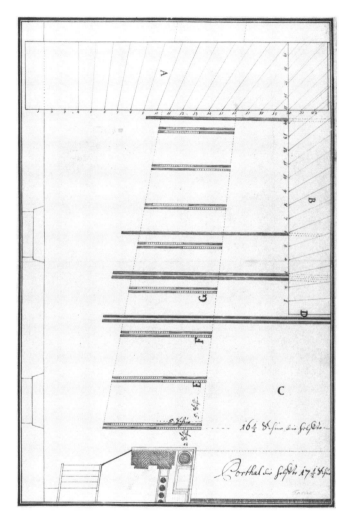

II. Half Ground Plan of a Stage Floor, undated

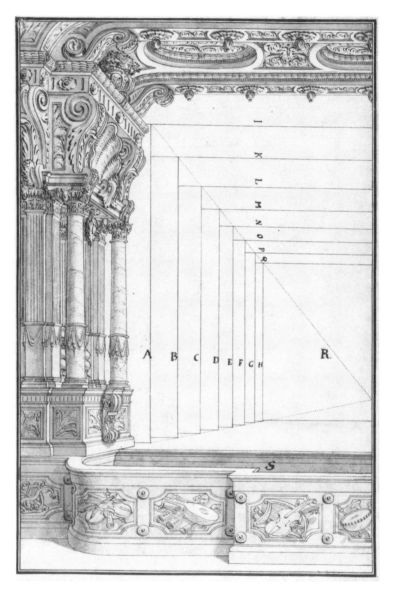

III. Proscenium with Perspective Lines Delineating Wings and Borders, undated

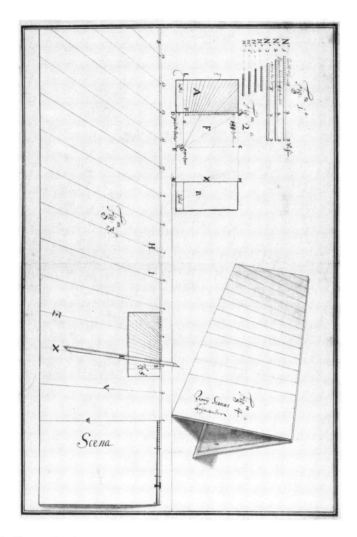

IV. Scema for Laying Out Perspective Lines on a Stage, undated

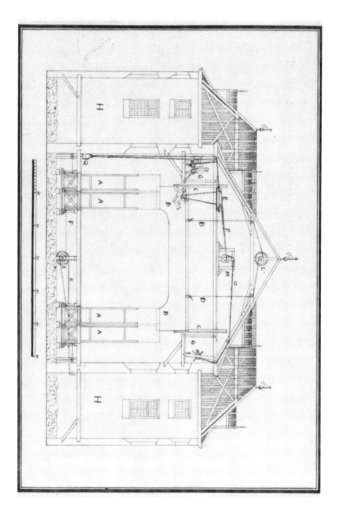

V. Cross Section of a Stage showing Wings, Borders and Fully
Rigged Flying Machine, undated

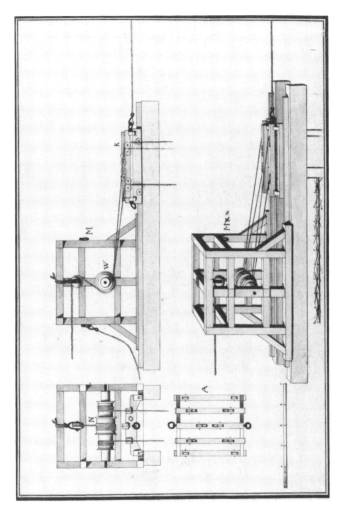

VI.   Details of a Flying Machine, undated

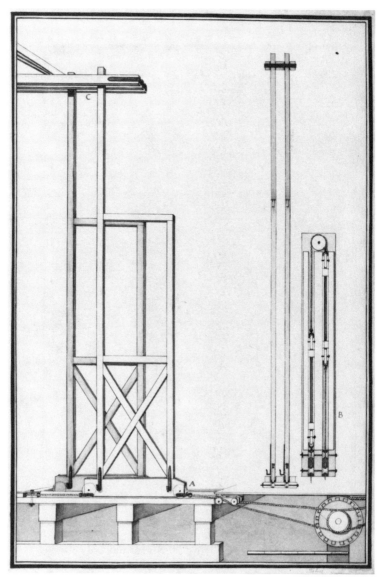

VII. An Order of Two Chariots, undated

VIII. Setting for a Room with Two Different Suggestions for the Decor, undated

IX. Fortified Town for *Alessandro nell' Indie,* 1749-1750

X. Tent Camp with Town in Background for *Alessandro nell' Indie,*
1749-1750

XI.   Ruins with Tent Camp in Background for *Alesandro nell' Indie,*
      1749-1750

XII. Open Space with Monumental Architecture, undated

ESSAY

ON THE ART OF CONSTRUCTING

THEATRES,

THEIR MACHINES AND THEIR OPERATIONS

By Citizen BOULLET
Machinist, Théâtre des Arts

In PARIS
At BALLARD'S, Printer and Bookseller for
the Théâtre des Arts,
Rue J.-J. Rousseau, No. 14,
and at the Salle de l'Opera

GERMINAL, YEAR 9
[1801]

English Translation By Cecil Thomas Ault Jr.
Ann Arbor, 1983

ESSAI

SUR L'ART DE CONSTRUIRE

LES THÉATRES,

LEURS MACHINES ET LEURS MOUVEMENS.

Par le C^{en}. BOULLET,

MACHINISTE DU THÉATRE DES ARTS.

SE TROUVE A PARIS,

Chez BALLARD, Imprimeur-Libraire du Théâtre des Arts, rue J.-J. Rousseau, n°. 14;

Et à la Salle de l'Opéra.

GERMINAL, AN 9. (1801.)

Table of Contents

As per the agreement passed between Citizen Ballard and myself, I place this work under the protection of the laws and probity of the citizens, and I shall sue in Court any counterfeiter or distributor who, in defiance of the existing laws and copyrights, would publish counterfeit editions.

The public is warned that the only authentic edition is the one which bears my signature.

Boullet

Paris, the 15th of Germinal,

Year 9.[1]

      Copies have been entrusted to the national library.

. . . . .

To:

Citizen Chaptal,

Home Minister

National Institute of the Sciences and Arts

Citizen Minister,

All the arts which flourish in a State have some influence on the public fortune. This truth is better appreciated when those in charge of their administration know how to direct their related activities for the benefit of society.

The art on which I am attempting to provide some instruction could be more useful. It dedicates its labors to the magnificence of theatre art,[2] whose reputation has always drawn foreigners to France, and it is their money, along with the government's, which contributes to the maintenance of the brilliance of a Theatre which is truly national. The patronage of those visitors attracted to this country by our arts will benefit industry, trade, and national funds.

It appeared proper to me, Citizen Minister, to publish under your auspices an essay which may prove useful to the *Théâtre des Arts*. It is to you that this art will owe the means for sustaining its success. It must raise itself to the highest degree of magnificence under a government from whose might Victory and Peace provide the means for endeavor and perfection.

Salutations and respect,

Boullet

Head Machinist of the

Théâtre des Arts

Paris, the 1st of Ventose, Year 9 of the Republic.[3]

Preface

In the course of the year 7,[4] a theatre newspaper which no longer exists prompted me to lay before the public some ideas on the dimensions of a large theatre, on the machines, the decorations and their configuration, the materials from which they are made, the motors that set them in motion to produce the various effects in an operatic performance, and on other theatres with machines. I believed that through developing my ideas I could render them useful, and I thought that forty years of work and experience at the great theatre of Versailles and at the Paris Opera should not be lost to those who may choose the same career. I received oral lessons on theory from my predecessors. I have had many and frequent opportunities to hear about and perfect practice. In this essay, I shall present the ways to overcome a great number of difficulties, and smooth the way which leads to the perfection of an art which is subjected more than ever to the demands of authors of operas and pantomimes, where all the resources of the machinist are necessary to produce marvelous effects.

No author has ever dealt with the importance of setting down theory in the construction of auditoriums, their configuration, dimensions and more importantly their relation and conformity to the stage. Each builder leaves it to the whim of his imagination which does not comprehend anything except those elements in all parts of the theatre which I have always thought should never infringe upon the most important one, which is to say, that which the public ought to see. It seems to me, in fact, that they are only concerned with motifs[5] for the various embellishments of theatre halls without troubling themselves about any of the particulars, or whether the whole stage can be seen well, free from any obstructions. In the theatres built in the past twenty years, I see nothing but evidence of no coherent theory, since all of them are different. In Paris, only one brings together the qualities of being able to see and hear well for the theatre goer. The famous architect, Peyre,[6] too soon snatched away from the arts,[7] made a great step towards perfection. However, by not following his example, the builders of most modern theatres have strayed far from the path laid out by this able master. This vainglorious egotism fares poorly and has greatly retarded the growth of the art.[8]

Perhaps it has not been fully understood that the size of the opening of the proscenium arch should determine all the other dimensions. It frames the tableau, and it can regulate and establish the locations from which the performers are seen, who, in their various places [on the stage] are truly the most important figures there.

I am far from believing that the art of the machinist is greater than that of the builder of comfortable and commodious halls. However, what I have to say of my art does not prohibit me from saying that the art of the theatre building is still in its infancy. Aided by lessons and advice from my master Arnout,[9] via many labors in the theatres of the court and town, I have managed to advance a few steps, but I owe that advantage to circumstances. The activities at the Opera have demanded extraordinary work for the past ten years.[10] Looking at it, one cannot appreciate enough what has to be done in the same day to set up and operate the scenery for a three act work and a ballet. The difficulties compound on a stage such as the one at the Opera, which when built was not created for that purpose, and on which the operation of the machines is continually hampered by obstacles which cannot be overcome without skill and experience.

I shall permit myself to say here that since one goes to the opera to see extraordinary things, there ought to be at the performance a theatre where the genius of an author's work is not thwarted by the impossibility of materializing his ideas.

The necessity of building an opera house on a carefully chosen site has been proven. Without doubt, circumstances alone have prevented the execution of various projects conceived to provide a clear stage for the marvels of the performance, security and ease for the audience, and to the government the glory of establishing and embellishing a kind of daily entertainment which out to be the object of curiosity and eager attention of foreigners.

If Peace, the protector of the arts, allows them in their just due, my wish is that this essay prove itself useful to those to whom the government will entrust the construction of an opera house.

Chapter I

GENERAL DIMENSIONS AND
PRINCIPAL CONSTRUCTIONS

In establishing the primary dimensions, I intend only to speak here of a theatre for grand opera. Everything to be discussed will be relative to such a building. I shall limit myself to some observations on principles applicable to other theatres.

My objective is to speak here of the dimensions, construction, and machines of the stage.

Later on, the theatre in general will be treated according to a sound theory which, I dare say, has not existed till now.

The first dimension from which all others are derived, including the stage and auditorium, is the width of the proscenium arch.

The width of the opening in the proscenium arch in an opera house is forty-three feet.[11] Following this given, the inside width of a stage from one lateral wall to the other should be twice the forty-three foot width of the proscenium arch plus one-fifth. This space is necessary to accommodate the operation of the scenery on both sides of the stage. In this space, the chorus, the supernumeraries and dancers can await their entrances without any personal danger and not be in the way of the machinists. The same height is required above the top of the proscenium arch as is the height of the proscenium opening itself, measured from the stage floor to the top of the opening,[12] and to be well proportioned, the proscenium arch should be eight-tenths as high as it is wide.

The rise beneath the roof is called the peak, and it is the highest part of the stage. The depth beneath the stage floor should be at least twenty-six feet.

With these dimensions, a set piece can be mounted from beneath the stage and another one hung from the grid.

The depth of the stage, that is to say the length from the back of the proscenium arch[13] to the back wall, should be twice the width of the proscenium arch. This length does not include the apron, which is the space between the front curtain and the footlights.

The above dimensions may seem extreme, considering the peak of the roof, but once I go into details of that part, it will be seen that the means of execution are practicable.

As the general dimensions for a large stage have been established, we shall now proceed with some important construction details such as the walls, the rafters, the floors in the stage house, those of corridors in the grid and the floors on the tie-beams, called the grid floors. These last mentioned beams support all the grid machinery and provide the supports for the counterweights of the same.

I shall also speak of the division of the stage into streets, whose arrangement should indicate the location of the rafters. The streets and rafters are still arbitrarily arranged and placed in no particular order. No one has ever considered that the machinist should be consulted by the builder and carpenter in the arrangement of these things.

The inside of a stage, such as the one here, is nothing more than a cage with four walls, the side containing the proscenium arch differing in its elevation from the other three.[14] These walls must be perfectly plumb, without any sloping, battering, projections or protrusions in any part.

Convenient stairs should be built from bottom to top in the four corners of this cage for servicing the machines and the various operations of the machinists.

Casement windows may be set into the foundation of this structure at the discretion of the architect and according to the exterior design of the building. However, it would be useful to consult the machinist in this matter, since the placement of the windows should be such as to provide daylight in the three parts of the stage house, namely the substage area, the stage itself, and the grid.[15] This is always useful when working. The grid should be lighted by skylights.

Having established these principles and executed these dimensions, the decorator[16] and the machinist can combine their efforts to produce what is expected of their art in the best possible conditions. Till now, these parts of the stage have been obstructed by cluttered surroundings and defective constructions, builders constricting the upstage space to provide dressing rooms for the performers or for store rooms. The stage is long and narrow and though space is provided for the performers, nothing is left over for operating the machines. The author of *Devin de Village* noted this, but his observations were ignored. Voltaire was more successful; when he spoke, the side benches disappeared and the stage was no longer obstructed by the dandies of those times.[17]

I must explain why the interior walls have to be perfectly plumb. This is necessary because the counterweights, which are sometimes very heavy, must descend very rapidly alongside the walls. If these walls are not plumb, the weights will swerve off their course, and if the walls slope, they will be damaged by friction. All the walls of the theatre must be made of brick; thus they will be fireproof. They must be at least seven feet thick at the foundation and six feet thick where they join the roof.

Of the three walls which enclose the stage house, it is the back or rear wall which demands the most care in construction because it is very high,[18] very wide and without any flooring to tie it in.[19]

The thickness of these walls may seem considerable, but one must consider what they support in the grid. By that I refer to the floors, both large and small, the machines, the dropcloths,[20] the bridges, the counterweights and the other equipment. Also, all the grid scenery and rigging are attached at this very high point in the stage house, creating constant shocks.

The placement of the streets or plans[21] of the stage determines the location of the rafters in the roof.

The streets on the stage should be six feet, four inches wide to be conveniently distributed. This distance will accommodate three chariots and two sloats. Therefore, the transverse supporting beams should be spaced twelve feet, eight inches apart, measuring from center to center. The center of the first beam must be determined, and it is the one nearest the second street.

Each street carries three chariots, or masts, which is what one calls the ladders which support the wings.[22] The masts are fifteen inches apart from each other. By locating the center of the first rafter one foot down stage of the first mast in the second street, as has been said and the remaining rafters twelve feet eight inches apart, center to center, all the divisions will come out properly in relation to the ground plan.[23]

This theory has never been used by any stage architect. Rafters, tie-beams and skeletal work are divided and arranged arbitrarily and once these theatres have been completed with such faulty planning, they are given to the machinist whom no one has consulted. Then it is said to him: "make marvelous things for us." By then, however, the simplest things are very difficult to execute. I repeat, without this theory, practice will bristle with problems and they will go on multiplying until one finds that he has nothing in the midst of plenty and plenty in the midst of nothing, and all of this the result of poorly calculated relationships between the streets and the supporting beams above and below the stage.

The framework for the roof of a large stage should be made with as little wood work as possible and yet be of the greatest strength and solidity since it supports all the dropcloths, bridges, and the roof, in addition to two machine floors, and it is absolutely necessary to have two machine floors in the peak of the roof. The many shocks which are the result of each scene change must also be taken into account.[24]

Such a framework should support 30,000[25] [27,270 pounds], and be constructed so that all the parts are "half flat"[26] in order to use little space. See the elevation of the rafters for the large roof in Plate I.

As one sees, such a roof must be much higher than ordinary roofs since two floors must fit into the peak. One is located on the main tie-beams, A, and the other on the second tie-beams, B, at a height of about ten or eleven feet above so that one can easily move about.

The roof peak must run longitudinally from the front to the back wall of the stage house. If it is peaked laterally, it will be impossible to work in the area by the back wall an it is in this area that one creates the grandest effects, such as storms, seas, and other practical effects. The effects created in this area are called "distant scenes."

The decorator and the machinist should not find any obstacles which might hinder the execution of their work. See the elevation and details in Plate II.

The skylights, C, (Plate I), should be planned in the grid so as to provide illumination for the two floors shown in that portion of the elevation.

The lower of these two floors, which is called a grid, rests on the main tie-beams as was mentioned above. It is called a grid because it has clear openings and the planks in the floor are regularly spaced apart from one another. It supports the pulleys, the cylinders or drums D, and the rope rigging. Suspended from its joists E, it also supports the pulleys for the dropcloths, the flying bridges F, and the fixed bridges G. The later corridors H, are also supported by it. Therefore, this floor requires a construction of the greatest strength. The following gives the materials which are used to make it and tells how it is done.

All the joists rest on the tie-beams at a regular interval of approximately two feet, nine inches, measured center to center. They are five to seven inches thick and the four faces are planed to square corners. They are set face-to-face on edge, since the pulleys for the various dropcloths are hung from them. Also attached to them are the hooks for suspending both the fixed and flying bridges. These joists are fastened to the tie-beams with hooks which keep them properly in place. Thus, even though they are firmly attached with the hooks, they can be moved if necessary. This method of arranging the joists on the tie-beams so they can be moved at will and still be secure is essential.

Here is how they should be set. Center stage is located on the tie-beam. A joist is set one-half inch on either side of the center line, leaving a space of one inch between the center joists. Then, measuring from center to center, the others are laid out as shown above at intervals of approximately two feet, six inches. The space between the center joists is called the "thumb"[27] and it always provides an open center line running up and down stage. If a joist were over the center line, one would always be drilling holes in it just to set and operate the various things which are used there.

Plumb to the lateral corridors of the grid, two joists which are stronger than the others are set on the tie-beams. They should not be less than seven inches by nine inches in size. They have a four inch space between them. The corridors will be suspended from these joists. They must be carefully chosen, since they not only support the corridors, but also the off stage ends of the fixed and flying bridges and all the pulleys which operate the dropcloths. Care should be taken to insure that the joists are perfectly aligned, center to center.

The joisting having been installed as indicated, the grid flooring is next. For this, strong fir planks are used.[28] These planks are set square to the joists, five-sixths of an inch apart from each other,[29] and are held lightly in place by nails as they must be removed often. They should be of the same width and the first one must run directly in line with the first street on the stage. By doing this, the machinist can always find a point for establishing the plumb to the streets below, even though the space above and below this floor is crowded with bridges, canvases, ropes, pulleys and so forth. This will make the work much easier when it comes time to set up the scenery.

The fixed and flying bridges are suspended from this floor. The fixed bridges made of fir are usually sixty feet long, fifteen inches wide, and two and one-half inches thick. They are supported by wooden yokes which are hung from the joists and firmly attached to them by iron stirrups. A bridge of this length cannot be made of a single piece, so the yokes should be set under the joints in the planks. Wooden handrails, or supports, are attached to the yokes on either side at a reasonable height. These bridges are usually suspended six feet below the joists of the grid. All the drops and borders[30] are hung, removed and adjusted from these fixed bridges.

The flying bridges are suspended only by rope yokes and the handrail is simply a rope stretched from one yoke to another. These yokes are suspended from the same joists as are the fixed bridges. They must be made as light as possible because in the course of a performance they are raised and lowered several times. They are made of fir planks, ten inches wide by one and one-quarter inches thick, tongued and grooved to fit into one another. When fitting the planks together, they should be aligned to a joist to make them stronger. The light tenders stand on these bridges at the beginning and end of the performance to attend the "ramps" or strip lights, on which candles are mounted inside of spring operated containers[31] to illuminate the ceiling pieces and borders. They are also used for emergency in case of fire.

As the joists of the grid floor, or grid, support all the dropcloths, ramps or strip lights, and the two kinds of bridges described above, creating much weight, one must be careful not to put the whole load on the same joists. This precaution is essential on a large stage. Because this simple rule has been ignored, I have seen joists break under their loads. This precipitates dangerous accidents and is difficult to repair.

We will now explain how the borders are rigged and hung. These cloths top off the scenery under the name of "ceiling pieces," for palaces and apartments, and "bands of air" or "skies" in other cases. They are stretched lengthwise on battens made of ash, and the batten is supported by as many lines as necessary. The number of lines is usually eight. They are attached to the joists of the grid or floor with iron snap hooks and the ring which goes into the hooks. The other end of the line is attached permanently to the batten. These lines are called "dead lines" or "false lines"[32] because they stay with the dropcloths and are never separated from them. They are used to adjust the dropcloths to the correct height. Once adjusted, they are left that way for whenever they are needed.

The grand drapes are the drops used for backgrounds as well as those used to adjust the height and width of the scene, and they are arranged in the same way as the borders.[33] The same is true for the act curtain.

The second grid floor is just under the peak of the roof and it is laid out on the second level of tie-beams. It is made into a grid similar to the previous one. In a large theatre, it ordinarily houses all the machines which move the borders for ballrooms or concert chambers which do not have to change very often. It houses drums, pulleys, winches, etc., just as the main grid does.

Chapter II

THE CORRIDORS OF THE GRID

In the preceding chapter I mentioned the lateral floor, or corridors. There are four of them, two on each side of the stage at different levels.

The first corridors *I* are thirty-one feet above the stage floor. They are raked in accordance with the rake of the stage so that the chariots in the streets, from the first to the twelfth, may pass beneath them. The second corridor *K* is at the level previously indicated. They are suspended on one side from the roof. The other goes into the wall and is secured there by iron anchors. All four need the greatest strength. Here is how they are built:

Between the two strong joists which were indicated to be four inches apart in the main grid, wooden supports, suspended from the joists, are mounted. They are approximately thirty-five feet long and five to six inches thick. Correctly spaced, they support the fixed ladders which are used to reach the different levels of the bridges and floors.

Once the supports are in place, the joists of these two lateral floors are assembled. Although they should be solidly constructed, they should be put together in such a way so that they can be easily removed. See Plate III, *A* and *B*. The joists of these floors should be five to six inches thick and covered with planks fitted with traps which may be lifted when needed.

The lowest of these corridors, *A,* is only used by the machinists who operate the machines and the lines or regulators which cause all the machines of this area [i.e., the grid] to move. All the grid machines are operated from this corridor since from this height the machinists can see what they are operating.

The second corridor *B* which is above the previous one, carries a much heavier load. It supports all the counterweights as well as their winches and attendant equipment. It is set fifteen inches further off stage than the floor beneath it. This distance is necessary to allow space for all the fixed ladders which allow access to the main grid and the various places above, as all the ladders should do.

There are strong wooden frames in these corridors which have cleats attached to them.[34] They are used for tying off the lines used to control all the operations in this part of the stage. See the details on drawing III, *A* and *B*.

If some doubts remain for the artist who wishes to acquire a knowledge of this particular type of construction, or if the amateur of mechanical arts is curious to pursue the array of works I am describing and has not found all the details here, I must warn him that there are too many details to compile in one essay. It will be a pleasure for me to give him explanations. They will be better understood on the stage where demonstrations are most forceful when the eye can see the real thing. My invitation for him to ask questions is already a pleasure; to answer them an obligation so as not to have wasted my many years of experience. This is my motive for writing. With this essay, I hope the machinist will acquire the necessary knowledge faster than was possible for me. I lost much time mastering technique and developing theory. It is my wish that my successors lose as little time as possible. The lack of direction in the arts is the source of unnecessary expenses which could be better employed for their advancement. Having spoken about the grid and its corridors, let us go down to the stage and talk about its main features. Next we shall speak about the construction of the stage floor and the relationship of the three parts of the stage: the substage area, the stage itself and the grid. Then we shall speak about the details of the machines, their parts, their equipment, their construction, and the required materials.

Chapter III

ON THE STAGE FLOOR AND THE TRAPS

The stage has two floors, the stage itself and one floor beneath it. See Plate IV, *A* and *B*.

The thirty-one foot space between the corridors above is empty except for some boxlike structures which run up and down the side walls. These are the counterweight chimneys, so-called because they look like chimneys. They provide the shafts in which the counterweights travel and they are attached to the walls from top to bottom with double sets of iron brackets which hold them securely. They are made of fir planks and they are fifteen inches square inside. Their location is determined by the position of the counterweights.

The floor of a large stage must be trapped in all its parts and still be built to provide the greatest strength. The greatest strain on this floor occurs when the troupe is performing on it, since the regularity of their tread causes every part to move.

This floor is made from fir planks,[35] and one and a quarter inches thick and very dry with no knots. If the wood is not dry, it shrinks and the joints loosen up. If there are knots, the soft wood around them wears down, leaving the knots to hurt the dancers' feet. This floor is made of small tables or traps which are three feet, eight inches square. Each trap is joined by two braces, four inches wide, which are set in and attached one and three-quarters inches from either side. This one and three-quarter inch space is the same thickness throughout so the stage will be as even as possible. The braces which join the traps must be planed very straight so they will fit well when they are opened and closed.

The other parts of the same floor are in the streets and consist of large and small slot traps. The small ones are used for the masts which pass through them to carry the wings. The large ones are used for the flat scenery which appears from beneath the stage. These larger ones are hinged and can be opened and closed as needed. These large and small slot traps are made of the same wood and their thickness is the same as for the regular traps. In order to strengthen them, they are reinforced with braces made of beech which are notched one-third of the thickness into the traps and firmly attached across the grain to the planks. Thus, these parts of the floor, though easy to move, are as strong as the ordinary traps. In this manner, in a space fifty feet wide and running the entire depth of the stage, no part of the stage floor is permanent. All of its parts are movable and may be arranged or changed as desired. The other parts of the stage floor, such as the space beneath the corridors and the apron, are permanent and may be constructed as any ordinary floor. Therefore, it is unnecessary to give any further details concerning them.

The traps are not only used as movable parts of the stage floor, but they have another function. They can disappear to create openings through which objects that have to rise from below can appear on the stage. They must do this by sliding to the right or left off stage under the other traps. In order to make this operation possible, the way to arrange them on the studs which support them is as follows:

The line indicated in Plate IV is called the center line. Starting at this line, measure out twenty-three feet on either side. At this point, the stud or joist supporting the floor is notched half its width and one and three-quarter inches deep, beginning at zero elevation and attaining its depth of one and three-quarter inches over a four foot length toward the center.[36] The notch in the supporting studs or joists, which support the flooring made into traps, is continued up to where they butt into the walls.

It is easy to see that the first trap panel on either side of the street is supported by a groove which slopes to a level one and three-quarter inches below the stationary part of the floor and thus sloped, continues into the one and three-quarter inch groove. Consequently, when that trap is pushed [off stage], it lowers itself and slides beneath the stationary flooring, as will the rest of the traps as they are likewise moved away from the center line or any other desired point of opening. When it is necessary to close them again, the traps are returned to their places by sliding them along the grooves prepared for them in the joists.

Let us speak, now, of the means of opening them, closing them, and resetting the first trap which was lowered. See Plate V, figures *1* and *2*. Beneath the floor, twenty-four feet, nine inches from the center (the slope is at twenty-three feet), a pinion *B* is attached to the studs *A* in which the pivot is set one and one-quarter inches off center, so that the lever *C,* which is attached to it, causes it to move one-quarter of a turn, thus raising and lowering it into the one and three-quarter inch groove as is required. After the operation, which is very simple to execute, a rope *D* is attached to the trap which is to be opened and is passed over the roller *E* which is set two feet away from the slope, which is to say twenty-five feet from the center. Then the traps are opened and closed manually.

Let us pass on to the details of the framework which supports all the floors of the substage area. We will then talk about chariots and masts which carry the decorations.

Chapter IV

ON THE FRAMEWORK WHICH SUPPORTS
THE STAGE FLOORS

The framework of the different floors beneath the stage must be made of oak which has been planed with a jointing plane. See plate I. The platforms L are set on the perpend stones M. Mounted on these platforms are the perpendicular posts N which support the joists of the first floor, as they rise. These posts are usually four to six inches thick and are eighteen to twenty-two feet long. They support the entire length of the stage floor, which is raked. The other floors run parallel to this rake. They are placed seven feet apart from each other, but none should be set beneath the center line of the stage. The joists which cap these posts, and which support those of the second floor, may be only five to six inches thick. They must be set on the flat side[37] and should span three posts. The joints of these joists should be cut perpendicular to the posts, and the joints should not all meet on the same rank of posts, since this is not a strong method of building.

The posts P which support the second or intermediate floor are fitted on the first joist. They are ordinarily four to six inches thick and six feet, nine inches long. They are fixed plumb, but centered on the joists to provide more support to the timber. They are capped with the joist Q which supports the rollment of the chariots for the wings. This joist must be five inches thick and seven and one-half inches wide. It is wider than the one below, since it receives the two rows of posts supporting the joists which bear the stage floor. The joints of these joists must meet plumb in the center of the support posts, since each one receives an iron track five-twelfths of an inch thick by one and three-quarter inches wide, which centered and runs their entire length to service the rollment of the chariots bearing the decorations. There, a groove, five-twelfths of an inch square, is cut to receive the track.[38] The posts which support the stage joists are fitted to the ones just described. There are twice as many of these as there are of those of the lower floors, and they are placed two by two, one next to the other, providing two rows of joists on each plumb, one of them being two and three-quarter inches thick, the other three inches, and all of them being five inches wide. As the stage floor rests on them, they must be dressed above in accordance with the slope of the rake. Those three inches thick receive the rabbets or slotting in which the traps run. The chariots for the wings run in the one and one-sixth space between these joists. The height from the top of the floor to the bottom of the joists is six feet. With such a dimension, a man can easily reach the underside of the traps. The support posts in this level of the floor must be four inches wide and one and three-quarters of an inch thick.

The joists R supporting the floor of the stage need particular care in the choice of wood to be used. As they are not very thick and are twenty-two feet long, they can be taken only from stout, quartered timber which is usually not very dry. If this is the case, these parts warp and their movement produces unevenness, which hampers work in that area. The setting and joining of these joists require the greatest of care. I have only spoken of the track joist which must be beneath a single chariot. A complete plan has three of them, one next to the other, and they are exactly alike. Therefore, it is seen that there are six joists in quite a narrow space. The first and last ones in each plan are three inches thick. They are the ones which hold the sides of the traps. The others are only two and two-thirds of an inch thick.

The space between each joist, which allows clearance for the chariots, is one and one-twelfth inches. The same space, which allows for the traps, is three feet, three and one half inches.

All the other streets, or plans of the stage, should be assembled in the same manner and chained together at the distances between them so that they are firmly affixed, keeping in mind, however, that this huge construction can be very quickly dismantled, piece by piece, if necessary.

As previously indicated, the platforms for all the framing rest on perpend stones, or cut stone blocks. I shall now explain how to install the framework.

The first frame, at the back of the stage is set at the indicated distance from the back wall and is fastened with iron clamps and screw lugs which are firmly secured in the wall. All the floor are dismountable, so all the clamps are movable. See Plate II, longitudinal elevation.

Here are the details and measurements in the width of a street or chariot plan:

	Feet	Inches
The first joist or beam, which is the one that receives the traps, is three inches thick		3
The space for the rollment of the chariot is one and one-sixth inches		1-1/6
The thickness of the second joist is two and three-quarter inches		2-3/4

The space for the large sloat between the two joists is eight inches		8
The third joist is two and three-quarter inches		2-3/4
The space for the rollment of the second chariot is one and one-sixth inches		1-1/6
The fourth joist is two and three-quarter inches		2-3/4
The space for the sloat between the two joists is eight inches		8
The fifth joist is two and three-quarter inches		2-3/4
The space for the third chariot is one and one-sixth inches		1-1/6
The sixth joist, which is the one that receives the other side of the traps, is three inches		3
Therefore, the layout of a street requires three feet and one sixth inch	3	0-1/6
For the opening of the traps, from one joist to the other, the space required is three feet, three and five-sixth inches	3	3-5/6
This gives a space for an entire street, from the front of one to the front of the next, of six feet, four inches	6	4

The intervals between the streets are maintained in the spaces in the traps by wooden cross-beams which serve as joists for all the floors, and are fastened between the joists with iron crampons, tightly secured into fixed brackets on these joists. The cross-beams are distributed in the appropriate number to receive the floors. The space between the traps, large and small, is held true with iron hooks attached to one another, forming a chain from the first frame to the last. The hooks must be very tightly secured into their lugs, since the slightest play can cause a general movement in the whole construction, including the floors, which is very dangerous. It is well understood that the hooks are turnable.[39] The chain which I have just described is for the first floor. There is another, just like this one, for every floor.

To erect the framework plumb would subject it to great disadvantages. The whole construction will be set one and one-quarter inches off plumb towards the back wall. If one ignores this essential precaution, the entire construction will tilt over toward the orchestra from the daily use of the stage and its heavy operations, due to its rake.

The lower floors in the elevation are made of tongued and grooved fir planks, firmly battened. They are no more than nine feet long, as it would be very difficult to handle such sections if they were longer, which when joined together form the floors.

Chapter V

ON THE CHARIOTS WHICH SUPPORT THE MASTS

Having completed the main constructions of the stage, the chariots are the first things to be considered.

There are three chariots for each plan, or street. The stage of the Opera has thirteen streets running from side to side. In giving the details for the construction of a chariot, I mean them to apply to others, since one looks like another. See plate VI.

The common width of a mast[46] is five feet, side to side, and the height is twenty-two to twenty-four feet. They differ amongst themselves according to their number of openings in the frame and profile.

The chariot consists of a strong pattern A, made from oak, eight feet long, eight inches wide and three inches thick. Into this patten are set four perpendicular posts B. The posts are three by five inches, with their height reaching from the top of the patten to the top of the joists in the stage floor. A cross-beam C, seven inches wide and three inches thick is set into the four support posts, two feet three inches beneath the underside of the joists. On either side of the chariot, these posts leave a space of five by three inches between themselves. It is in the space D that the part E of the mast is placed. These four posts are secured at the top by two iron straps F, one on either side. They are mounted one inch below the bottom of the joists of the stage floor and fastened with nuts and bolts. The ends of the four posts, that is to say those parts of them which extend above the iron straps, are notched one inch to create a tenon on top.

The tenons pass between the joists of the stage floor, and these joists are one and one-sixth inches apart. The tenons keep the chariots and masts upright as they move. The tenons on the heads of the chariot are necessary to keep it between the joists. Another precaution to be taken is to regularize and fix the course line of the patten. This is derived from its length with regard to the perpendicular line which is indicated by the center of the tenon, taken from its height. On each end of the patten, a brass[41] wheel G is installed which is twelve inches in diameter and has a groove in its circumference which is one and one-sixth inches deep. This groove runs on the iron track H, which has been set into the joist of the lower floor and the wheel rolls on it.

It is necessary to explain why I set the depth of the groove at one and one-sixth inches. When the chariots move very rapidly, a great jolt occurs when they come to a stop. This jolt can disengage the wheel from the iron track. Then the trouble of resetting it costs the machinists time, and time is governed by the orchestra, which controls the entire opera.

I have rendered these accidents impossible, and one will easily see how.

It will be remembered that the posts of the chariots described above each have a one-inch thick tenon at the top, which runs between the joists of the stage floor. Also, the thickness of these posts is three inches, which leaves an excess of two inches cut beyond the tenon. By making this cut two-thirds of an inch beneath the joist no amount of rocking can disengage the wheel, because the wheel, having a one and one-sixth inch groove in it, and the head of the chariot having only two-thirds of an inch play between the cut in it and the joist, (the chariot's space to rock only being two-thirds of an inch) one-half inch remains and that is enough to prevent the wheel from disengaging from the track, being held by the one-half inch. Without this precaution, they can rock or lurch and this can cause a "false stop." When this happens, the chariot and wing will not move into position.

Each end of the patten is bound with an iron strap J to which a snap hook is attached that receives the ring of the line that conducts the motivating energy from the counterweight.

I shall speak of such lines later and show how to rig and use them when I discuss the operations.

The chariots are always located beneath the stage and the masts. The latter are mounted in the chariots and they are sometimes called "false wings" since they are not decorated. They carry the decorated wings or leaves of decor.

The masts are five feet wide and eighteen to twenty-four feet tall. They are made of the two stiles K, which are five inches wide and three inches thick. Their lower parts extend three feet into the chariot. One foot above the level of the stage an oak rail, six inches wide and three inches thick is set into them. At the top are two horizontal braces of oak, which are only four inches in breadth, and they are spaced one foot from each other. There is a horizontal brace at the bottom and between it and the lower brace at the top is a space of about seventeen feet, depending on the graduated heights of the masts.[42] This space is used on the back of the mast for an eight-inch wide ladder M which is built there for climbing to the top of the mast to fasten the decorated wing. The wing is fastened by one of its cleats with a rope. These masts should be very easy to remove from the chariot. The two large stiles of the mast, that is to say the two pieces which fit into the chariot, are reduced to a one-inch thickness along the portion which fits into the chariot. See Plate VI, figure one. However, as a board so thin will be too weak, this entire part is reinforced by an iron strap which is passed around the reduced portion and continues four feet above the level of the stage floor. These straps are solidly attached with nuts and bolts. The faces inside the mast are notched one foot above the level of the stage floor, making a mortise to receive the bottom horizontal brace L.

These masts should be easy to set in and remove from the chariots, but with very little play. With what I have said, the details on Plate VI are sufficient.

Chapter VI

ON THE MACHINES, THEIR OPERATIONS, AND
HOW TO FIT THEM OUT

Having completed these first constructions, the stage is prepared
to receive the machines. We are going to talk about the way to equip
them, how to make them move, and how to calculate their performance, according to their effect. Here is where the necessity for good
practice appears, and it will be correct only as much as it is based on
a good theory.

It should be remembered that the structures beneath the stage
are divided by streets and by various levels of floors, and that this
entire structure rests upon perpend stones or foundation blocks, and
finally that the first elements of this structure are platforms.

It is above these platforms that the axles will be set which will
receive the drums that make everything move when they respond to
the motivating force of the counterweights.

It is usual to set an axle[43] in the bay formed by the space between
the two support posts. (Plate VII, figure *A)* It is usually this axle
which sets the wings in motion. Such a movement is called a "shift."[44]

The other axles are likewise set into the bays; however, every
other one is left vacant. Thus streets are created for moving quickly
from one working area to another.

It is seen that once the center axle is placed, the bays to the left
and right are free. The other axles are placed to the left and right in
the other bays as long as there is one, while leaving one bay empty.

All of these axles are of unequal lengths, and they should be eight
to nine inches square.

Let us determine the lengths. The main axle which will move the
wings should be set into the outside support beams of the first street
and extend to opposite outside beams on the other side of the sixth
street. (Plate VII, figure 2) Therefore, it will be thirty-two feet long,
and is suspended along its length by two bearings. Without these
bearings it would bow under stress and stop turning.

The axles should be placed in the other bays in the following
manner: All begin on the outside support beams, centered therein, of
the first street. They continue, the one of the right running from the
outside support beam of the first street to the opposite outside beams

of the third, the one on the left, still centered, from the front to the back of the fourth, and thus the rest of the axles continue to the back wall.

These axles should intersect a street, one ahead and one behind. Their joints should always be set on one side or the other of the street, or there will be no place left for the lines to be attached to the drums.

All of these axles should be made of unhewn oak,[45] which is very straight and very dry so there will not be any apprehension about their use. If they break down or become unserviceable it will be difficult to replace them when all the machinery has been installed in the other parts of the theatre.

In the old days, they were made with eight sides. That cannot be as good as the square, which should be adopted in preference to a circle, which the eight-sided ones approach, since the drums which are mounted on these axles will be supporting great weight as they turn.

Making them exactly square is indispensable for convenience and ease in calculating and fixing the different diameters.

In squaring them, the wood is removed evenly and little by little from each side so that the operation does not create what is called a "split." That would be a very serious defect.

After the axle has been planed, the four paces are prepared. After it has been cut to the desired length, the ends are lined to find their centers.[46]

Both ends are ferruled. The diameter of the ferrule will be equal to the width of the square axle, and it will be of good iron, five-twelfth of an inch thick by two inches wide. After having joined joined it to the axle with a mallet, it is secured with screws whose heads are flat and countersunk. Then, an iron gudgeon or trunnion is driven into each end. The gudgeon penetrates one foot, leaving at least two inches protruding. The protruding part will have been turned round on a lathe. The part inside will be squared.

After it has been driven in with a mallet, it is secured with an iron key which passes through both the axle and the gudgeon. (Plate VIII, figure one) That is how the drum axles are prepared with their iron fittings.

The two ends of the axle are supported by horizontal side beams, which are solidly affixed to the support posts of the frame, where they meet. Usually they are notched one inch and secured with two bolts at either end. This side beam is as long as the distance, or reach, from one support post to the other, [which is] eight feet, outside to outside measurement, and is six inches by ten inches thick. Centered is an opening which will receive the gudgeon. It is fitted with a cushion or bearing of brass which seats the entire fixture at the base of the bushing, which will receive the axle.

The round fitting which is the same diameter as the axle and into which the latter is fitted is called a bushing. It has a depth of one and one-half inches, and the gudgeon fits into it. The axle has been fitted into the gudgeon so it will not jam while turning on the cushion inside the bushing. Only the gudgeon has to be replaced and not, as I have seen, the entire jammed movement, not to mention the embarrassment of such an accident.

A cylinder or drum axle which is more than twelve feet long cannot be supported by just two bushings. It must be given extra support by a collar which is set into the midpoint of its length. Here is how to make collars. See Plate VIII, figure two.

Two pieces of wood *A* are assembled side by side like side beams. Their length is sufficient to reach from one support post to another, and they are fitted to the support posts just as if they were side beams. Then a round cut is made at the center point between the two of them. This cut *B* is two inches greater in diameter than the diameter of the axle which is to be set into it. Then, five cylinders *C* or roller bearings of brass, three inches long and of the same diameter, are set into the cut. The half cut in each piece of wood is called a lunette. When mounted, their inner circumference is the same as the diameter of the axle where it is rounded and bound with the ferrule which turns on the bearings *E* in the collar at point *D*. Another way to make roller bearings is to have them roll around the axle, but this becomes very expensive and machines for the theatre are not heavy enough to require such demanding methods.

Everything that has been explained about the axle and its hardware applies to all the machines of this type, whether on the stage or in the grid. Therefore I shall not return to these details again when I speak of axles in the cylinders and drums.

Having just arranged the grand drum to move the wings and I have, one might think that it is ready to burn. However, it is only nine inches thick and therefore only the core for those things which will be built around it, and they are actually what one calls cylinders or drums. The purpose of the grand drum is to move the wings and thus effect their changes on the right and left side of the stage.

As all of the wings do not have the same distance of track to travel, and since each has its own line, the axle must be built to the appropriate size for each place in the arrangement of the chariots. Furthermore, the height from which the counterweight falls to make the axle turn must also be calculated.

The chariot which has the greatest distance to travel moves fifteen feet and the counterweights fall forty feet. The drum will be made with three different sections which will have two different diameters: one foot, eight and three-quarter inches to receive the motor lines, and four feet, five and one-quarter inches for the counter-weight line. This creates a mechanical advantage of two to one.

Having moved along, a few terms should be explained, such as drum, line or motor drum, and counterweight drum. In general, any thickness on an axle is called a drum. The terms "line drum" or "motor drum" are used when referring to a drum whose lines cause other things to move. The counterweight drum is the one which makes the axle move. It transfers the load to the counterweight, which supplies the power.

The lines which are attached to the counterweight drum are called counterweight drum lines. There are two types. The first is a hand operated line which runs to the drum. It is called a "regulator line" or simply "regulator." The other is always attached to the counterweight and it is called the counterweight line. However some regulators run directly to the counterweight and others to the counterweight drum. One should refer to both of them as governors. In effect, one governs the load when it is released and the other counterweight when it is raised.[47]

It is important to pay close attention to the use of the following:

1-Motor drum,
2-Counterweight drum,
3-Counterweight drum line,[48]
4-The regulator.

One should also know how the counterweight line is connected to its drum and remember that since this line provides the power, it must work counter to the load in order to move or release it.

Before demonstrating how these drums work, it should be explained how they are constructed, how the lines are rigged to them, and also how the other rigging is used.

Once the length and diameter have been determined, the axle is laid out with divisions from one end to the other. See Plate VII, figure two. On each of these divisions a round plate A is mounted. The plate is of the proper diameter and it is made of beech. It is one and one-quarter inches thick so it will hold the nails well. The plate is attached to the axle with wooden battens when the diameter of the former is not too large. Plates with large diameters are attached with angle irons. Then these plates are covered with fir staves. They are rounded off on the outside and suitably curved on the inside. Care must be taken that these staves are exactly centered when they are attached; this gives them their whole strength. They are attached very tightly next to one another.

Just before the last stave is to be nailed in place, care is taken to attach short lines to the axle at various intervals. These lines protrude through the staves to the outside of the drum and they are called "prisoners." They provide an excellent means of attaching whatever type of line is desired to the drum. Without these prisoners, the lines would have to be attached with nails. That method is not strong and the drums are soon broken up by the nails.

Let us pass on to the winches, their description, and their use. Stage winches are second degree levers. Properly speaking, they are the arms of the men who operate them. They serve to raise the weights which in turn will move such and such a load when they are set free to descend to their resting places according to the disposition of their rigging.

Let us explain what a stage winch is. See Plate IX, figure one. It is an axle made of oak five feet long by eight inches thick. A two inch width is rounded off either end, and each end is ferruled and gudgeoned like the grand drum described above. At the two places where the square portion of the axle ends, right next to the rounded parts, levers or blades, made of fir, measuring three feet from the center of the axle, are set in. The handles of these levers should be spaced twenty-one inches apart from each other. If the distance is greater, the men who operate them will lose strength by overextending their arms. On the other hand, if the space is less, the job will take too long.

These levers or blades are mounted on the axle between two circular plates of a suitable size. These plates, just as the levers, are joined together with nails and joined to the four faces of the axle with tenons. They are secured by four angle irons. These levers are fourteen in number. I have noticed that ordinarily these levers are joined to the plates with nails, but it is better if bolts are used. If a lever breaks, it is easily repaired. This cannot be done so well if one uses nails.

The necessity of being well understood requires that I explain the blocks, rollers, and cleats in details. The uses of these pieces of stage equipment should be familiar to the machinist who wishes to improve himself. Once known, it will also satisfy the curiosity of those to whom the arts are an inspiration and a joy. I also believe that the lover of the theatre will find some pleasure in understanding the works of the machines and the scenery whose effects have earned his applause. A block is a piece of wood pierced with a hole in which a sheave is secured athwart with an iron pin.

There all sizes of blocks. The smallest have sheaves three inches in diameter (Plate IX, figure two) and are made of walnut. There are some fifteen inches in diameter and even larger. These are made of brass and are set three into one block for the counterweight lines.

The blocks used to operate glories have block housings like the others and the sheaves, nine inches in diameter and one inch thick, are made of guiacum.[49] The lines which pass through these blocks are made of brass rope. These lines, which get smashed when running on brass, are not exposed to this danger when running on guiacum, which is still hard enough to bear the weight of a glory. From the friction of turning, the hole through which the axle passes will wear away, so a brass bushing is set in the sheave and the whole thing is turned on a lathe.

A fixed roller is a piece of oak or any other hard wood, eight or nine inches thick and rounded. Its length is determined by where it is installed. These rollers do not run and are very firmly secured. Running the entire length of the lower corridor in the grid, there is a row [of these] attached to the main support posts. The regulators which operate the drums and counterweights are passed around these rollers. They are installed so that their height is one foot above the corridor floor. At this height, the machinist has one foot set firmly on the roller, and he can thus manage a considerably heavy load. Around this roller the lines pass one or one and a half turns at most. By playing out the line more or less rapidly, the movement of the particular load is accelerated or slowed down.

Above the roller, and four feet above the corridor floor, is an oak beam, seven inches wide and five inches thick, which runs parallel to the roller and is attached to the main support posts with iron bolts. The cleats for the lines are attached to this beam. The cleats are made of hard wood, sixteen inches long, four inches wide, and two inches thick. They are notched one-half inch, as is the beam, and are held in place by two bolts. Here I note that everything which is to be used on the stage, including all of its parts, should be joined with bolts, since a bolt is easily dismounted and likewise removed. All the moving machinery and stage equipment should be very strong and yet capable of being very quickly and easily disassembled. It is to these cleats that the lines which pass around the rollers will be secured for [the use of] the machinist who controls the movement of the machinery. He turns the line twice around the cleat, securing the last turn with a half-hitch.

The blocks used beneath the stage are like those used in the grid. The rollers are just as strong and are mounted to the joists of the first floors. Their length is the same as the width of the street. The cleats for the lines, like those of the lower corridor, are set into a beam which is sufficiently strong and mounted on the two support posts of the grid framing. These lines are rigged just like those in the grid.

Chapter VII

ON THE MACHINERY WHICH CHANGES
THE SLIDING WINGS BY DRAWING THEM INTO
VIEW OF THE AUDIENCE

Remember that the cylinder or drum which regulates this shift is ready to go. Suppose, then, that the chariots are also ready with their masts and painted wings, and that a line is attached to the patten of the chariot with a ring, and that the other end of that line is attached to the drum. The counterweight drum has also been rigged with its counterweight, which is a type of primary motor. Now everything is ready to move if sufficient force is used. See Plate VII. The force comes from the counterweight. We will now turn our attention to these counterweights and the winches which are used to raise them.

It was stated above that the winches were located in the main machine floor and second corridor of the grid. The winches under discussion here are in the substage area, since the machinists who make this shift work down there even though the counterweights rise to a height of forty feet.

A rope is attached to the winch B^{50} and it is secured by running it many times through the levers on the winch. The other end of the rope is passed through the pulley C and fastened to the arbor shackle of the counterweight D with a ring which is on the end of the rope. The pulley C has two sheaves made of brass, which are at least one foot in diameter. The winch line is passed through one of the sheaves. It is used to raise the counterweight. The counterweight line is passed through the other. One end of it is attached to the counterweight D and the other is attached to the drum A, to the counterweight which one either wants to move or keep motionless.

Ropes running from the counterweight are usually one and a half inches thick. Their lengths are determined by the distance from the drums to the counterweights. A one and a half inch rope support two thousand weight, [1,811 pounds] without danger.[51]

A counterweight consists of an arbor made of well tempered iron, five to eight feet long and one and one-quarter inches thick. It is terminated at the bottom by a strong button-shaped base which holds the weights when they are stacked on the arbor. At the top of the arbor is a "head" which is slightly over two inches wide and has a hole in it to receive an iron pin which connects the shackle to the counterweight. See Plate VIII, figure three. The shackle is shaped like a loop. The pin can be removed and put back into the hole as needed. The lead weights which are stacked on the arbor are ten inches in diameter and two and a half inches thick. They ordinarily weight one hundred *livres* [90.09 pounds]. They are slotted wide enough along the radius to allow them to pass around the shaft of the arbor. A small ridge around their circumference makes them easy to grip with the fingers when lifting them (figure four).

Sometimes in the course of a performance a counterweight must be used many times without always remaining loaded with the same amount of weight. Therefore, fifty *livre* weights [45.045 pounds] are also provided for this purpose. They are shaped like the other ones, but the lighter weight makes them easier to load and unload, (figure five).

Before shifting the scenery, we should discuss all the details of this operation as well as the machines and their parts. We have already said that a chariot only has a maximum of fifteen feet to travel. However, twelve on each side must be moved simultaneously, as six advance while six withdraw. This is how it is done. See Plate VII.

The leading chariots are moved up to the stop cleat E. Then the back line G is passed around the back pulley F. This line is one inch in diameter and has a ring attached to each end of it. Each of these rings is attached to the hooks H which are mounted on the pattens of the chariots bearing the masts. Thus, one sees that as one chariot is drawn forward, the other is withdrawn. From the hook I, pass the ring of the line K over the roller L and run it over to the drum A. There it is attached to one of the prisoners which were put there for that purpose.

This operation is repeated for the rest of the chariots. The lines are run successively from the hooks of one chariot to another.

The hauling path is a little oblique when the chariot is hooked up from the center, but that affects the hauling and resistance very little. The back lines are also changed on each street, depending on which chariot is to be advanced. Also, a roller M is needed in the space between each large slot. See Plate VII, figure three. This roller should be easy to remove.

When all the dozen motor lines are affixed to the drums, the operation should be readied. To do it correctly, the counterweight line N has one end attached to the shackle of the counterweight, while the other end is passed through one of the two sheaves C which is adjacent to the counterweight sheave. Then it is run over to the counterweight drum A.[52] There it is passed around once in the opposite direction of the other lines and attached. On the same drum, the regulator *O* is given four turns and attached. After that, the other end of the same line is passed around the fixed roller *P,* indicated beneath the stage.[53]

When the lines are attached to the chariots, turned four times around their drums, it is obvious that the force of the descending counterweight will move the chariots. Then, in order to move the withdrawn chariots forward, it is necessary to re-raise the counterweight while likewise turning the drum to slacken the lines. This is accomplished by taking in the regulator *C* as the counterweight rises. When the counterweight is taken all the way out, the motor lines *K* which are unhooked and moved to be hooked to the chariots which are next to be moved. The regulator is tied off to the cleat, just as has been said. As the regulator is wound around the drum in the opposite direction of the counterweight line, the drum is held fast between the two, unable to move.

In order to free the drum, the moment the shift is ordered, the winch *B,* which raised the counterweight and holds it suspended, is released and the force of the weight shifts to the counterweight line, which runs to the drum. Hence, that line bearing the weights will cause the drum to turn as long as it is not restrained by the regulator which is wound around the drum in the opposite direction. Thus it is that by releasing the regulator, the descending counterweight will cause the drum to turn and its movement will heave on the lines attached to the withdrawn chariots, causing them to advance.

This operation is repeated every time one wants to make a shift.

There are still other details to be shown, such as methods which will allow that the chariots do not all stop at the same distance, that others should only advance. But it would be superfluous to study such simple things whose practice and execution are so easy.

Chapter VIII

ON THE INTERMEDIATE FLOOR BENEATH THE STAGE

On this level of the floor, only those things which will appear through the sloats will be found. Otherwise, it is clear for its entire width of fifty feet.

Twenty-five feet on either side of the center, a row of drums is installed between the last pairs of support posts. They are at the height of the perpend stones and they are identical to those described for use with the chariots.

As the pitch of this floor follows the rake of the stage, and it is absolutely necessary for a drum to be level, a drum can only span two streets. Also, it is necessary to set the drums so that one end is at the beginning of a street and the other end at its termination. See the longitudinal section in Plate II.

This row of drums is used for raising the traps, ground rows, individual trees, and the lighter pieces of scenery. The arrangement of these drums should be the same as that for the drums down below. The rigging, the motor drums, the counterweight drums, the pulleys, and everything else is likewise the same, and it is all arranged to service the particular area where it is installed. All one has to do is attach a line to one of the drums.

Chapter IX

ON THE FIRST LEVEL BENEATH THE STAGE FLOOR
WHERE THE TRACKS
FOR THE CHARIOTS ARE LOCATED

All the operational equipment for the machines in the substage area is located on this floor. The machinists move about their variously assigned stations to hook up a chariot, to release a line, or to open and close the traps and sloats.

This floor (See Plate IV, *R)* extends from one wall to the other in order to provide the necessary space for withdrawing the traps and chariots, and to facilitate the arrangement of the many accessories for the scenery that one must have on hand during a performance.

The machinists who work in the substage area perform all their operations on this floor because it is the only level beneath the stage where they can have daylight and fresh air.

The hooks which form the chain to hold the whole structure of the stage together are seen there.

The iron tracks which are used for the chariots are mounted on the joists beneath this floor. The horizontally mounted pulleys which are necessary for shifting the chariots are also mounted on these joists.

Chapter X

ON THE FLATS AND OTHER KINDS OF SCENERY
WHICH APPEAR FROM BELOW

Unlike a curtain, which ripples in the air as it descends from the grid, a flat[52] is a piece of scenery which is mounted on a frame and set level to the stage floor. A flat can be just ordinary, or it can be pierced with openings such as doors or colonnades.

No matter what it represents, a flat must be adapted to the mountings which will be used to lift it quickly and smoothly from below. The mounting consists of three fir boards which are joined together to form a sliding beam. See Plate X, *A.* The sliding beam is about thirty feet long, five inches wide, and four inches thick. On either side of the sliding beam there is a three-quarter inch groove to allow space for a rope.

These sliding beams run in fourteen foot long conduits which are called cassettes. The cassette *B* has a sheave mounted on either side of the sliding beam. They are in the enlarged part at the top which is called the head. The head is held in place by iron bands which are wrapped around it. The upper band has two iron pins which protrude upwards on the back side. They are used to mount it in the sloat.[53]

The sheaves in the head should be made of brass and they should be fitted with pins, not bolts. The pins should hold the sheaves very well and allow them to turn freely in their bushings. See Plate X, figure two.

When the cassettes are mounted in the sloats, the upstage side of the sliding beam *(A,* figure two) is one-quarter of an inch away from the joist *C.* Their location is determined by the shape and width of the decoration or flat they carry. Having determined their location, two holes are drilled in the underside of the joist *C* to receive the two pins, *(D,* figure 2), which protrude up from the iron band of the cassette. Then the cassette is fitted into the holes, which hold it in position but do not support it. To support it, wooden braces are set on the joist *E,* which support the base of the head *F.* It is seen that by this method the head of the cassette can neither lower itself nor move side to side.

It is necessary that the cassette be absolutely plumb.

It is attached lower down to the first joist by iron brackets and screws.

Having mounted the cassettes, a line is attached whose ring is affixed to the bottom of the core (A, figure two). Then the line is passed through one of the two sheaves B, depending upon which one leads to the drum, and the sliding beam is slid into the conduit. Care is taken to run the line properly into the grooves of the sliding beam.

It is easy to see that by pulling on the lines G, the sliding beam A will rise, and so it is with the others. Sometimes as many as six are found in the same street, which is troublesome when it comes time to attach the lines to the drums. It is best to avoid such practices as much as possible so things are not piled up on top of each other.

Having carefully assembled the cassettes with their sliding beams, mounted them in the sloats, and rigged them with their lines, it is now necessary to mount the flat on the sliding beams. This prepares the decoration to be raised and lowered and here is how it is done.

First, the sliding beams are raised to height in which they will be used in their "up" position. The flat is mounted on the bottom to them with nuts and bolts. When the flat or decoration which is to be used is clamped to the sliding beams, they are raised so the piece is three inches above the stage floor. Then the holes for the bolts are drilled through the flat and the sliding beam. The bolts are pushed through from the up stage side and the heads seat into the sliding beam. The nuts are fastened on the front of the flat. By raising the flat, it is easier to crank the drill when making the holes for the bolts.

When the lower bolts have been set in the flat, each one of the lines G which operate the sliding beams is attached to the drum H and wrapped around it as many times as necessary to lower the flat.

It should be noted here that since drums are used, it is impossible for all the lines running to the cassettes to be the same length. Here is where experience is valuable and has something to teach. First, take the longest line and tighten it around the drum as much as possible. Then do the same with the next longest and the next in order until the last or shortest is done.

This precaution is just a very close approximation and does not satisfy machinists for whom theory prescribes precise calculations. However, these lines conduct the power from the movement of the drum to the object which is set in motion. The material from which they are made renders them very susceptible to stretching, depending on the weight of the load. Their tension should be adjusted in a way that experience has shown to be best.

Weather affects the length of ropes. I have seen ropes vary as much as three feet over a seventy-two foot length, from a humid to a dry day. These variations are responsible for the annoyance of the scenery's not appearing to be properly trimmed, since the operation of the machines is affected by the amount of moisture or dryness in the rigging.

When all the lines are attached to the drum, the regulator J is wrapped around the counterweight drum and attached to the prisoner or loop. Since the drum is free, the regulator is played out and the flat is lowered to a convenient level for attaching the next row of bolts. Only three [rows of bolts] are used on a piece twenty-seven feet high.

It is advisable to do the bolting operation as close to the stage floor as possible and to insure that the sliding beam is lined up exactly in the center of the cassette. Having finished the second row of bolts, the piece is lowered again replaying out the regulator until the level for the third row of bolts is reached.

Then, the piece is lowered to a level so the top stands one foot beneath the stage floor. At the bottom of the flat where it reaches its lowest point, a batten called a "stop cleat" is attached to the support posts. By doing this, not only the "up" but the "down" position is controlled. Let us now pass on to the operation which will raise the flat and cause it to appear promptly into view of the audience.

The counterweight L is raised as high as needed. All the slack which is let out by the counterweight line K is taken up by the counterweight drum H until the line is taut. Then the drum is made fast. The regulator I is wrapped around the same drum in the opposite direction. The counterweight line K is charged with the counterweights and now nothing inhibits the drum from turning except the regulator which restrains it. Then, at the appointed moment, the regulator, which in every instance is a governor, is let go and everything moves according to plan.

I must make one very important comment here on the operation of the counterweights. When they weight eighteen hundred to two thousand *livres,* [1,636.2 to 1,818.0 pounds], they should be rigged in such a way that they hit the ground at the end of their course. Without this precaution, the stopping jolt will break the lines.

Using the methods and operations I have just described, everything can made to rise from beneath the stage into view of the audience: flats, trees, shrubs, ground rows, etc. In every case a force is applied to overcome a resistance.

To make the piece redescend, all one has to do is change the load so it is carried by the regulator, and it is on the same side of the drum as the motor lines. Therefore, it must be reversed on the drum, given a turn, and tied off at the cleat. Then the counterweight line is disconnected from the drum, and when the regulator is let out, the flat will return to the stop cleat where it rested before it rose.

Chapter XI

WHAT SHOULD BE DONE ON THE STAGE
SINCE IT IS THE MAIN AREA

This part is a floor whose length extends from the footlights to the back wall. Its width is from one wall to the other. In this direction it is level. The stage is raked and rises three inches per *toise*[54] [i.e., one-half inch per foot] along its length. (See Plate II)

It is slotted in every street or plan, and these openings allow passage for the chariots to move the wings. (See Plate IV, *B)* In the off stage areas, right and left facing the large support posts for the beams in the grid, light wooden frames are built which create cubicles. They are seven feet wide and built beneath the main corridors. They are used for open-view scene docks and the wings for each setting will be stored in each one of them.

At the rear of the stage a corridor or hallway is also built. It is six feet wide and eight feet height so armed soldiers can pass each other easily, and it runs all the way from one side of the stage to the other, stopping on either side at the plumb line of the overhead corridors. This hallway is a thoroughfare from one up stage corner of the stage to the other and is absolutely indispensable. Just above this corridor, several little balconies are built onto the back wall, *(F,* Plate II). They are six feet, six inches deep and six feet, six inches above one another. They are strong enough to hold all the dropcloths, borders and draperies which are stored there. They are stored there in family by family [i.e., complete settings], so they will not be confused with one another and so one will know where to find them when they are needed.

I observed earlier that the stage should be clear except for the counterweight chimneys and the four service stairs. Every other kind of construction is a nuisance in this area and should not be permitted. When I speak on setting up a scene, it will become clear just how valuable these open spaces on the sides of the stage can be.

Chapter XII

ON WHAT A WING IS, ITS CONSTRUCTION
DIMENSIONS AND HOW TO USE IT
ON THE STAGE

An ordinary wing, which is to be covered with a painter's canvass, is eight feet wide and twenty-seven feet high. It is made of stiles and rails[55] of fir. A thin strip of wood, or profiling piece, is attached to the on-stage side of the wing, and it is used for making contours which give the wing its general outline.

The wing is never assembled with mortise and tenons because they would be difficult to repair if they should be broken. It is assembled with notched lap joints and fastened with nails.

Care should be taken to set the notch of the rail on the back and not the front. Otherwise the grip who climbs up the mast to fasten the wing might pull the rail off. If he should do this, he would fall from a great height and bring the piece down with him.

The canvas is attached to the wing with tacks and it is trimmed one inch inside the edge of the wing. If it is set any closer to the edge, the grip will tear the canvas for want of a place to put his fingers while gripping the wing.

When the tacking is done, the entire back of the canvas is covered with grey paper to give better strength, to cover any holes, and to arrest the transparency, since if lights are seen through the wings, the illusion is damaged for the viewer.

A wing weighs about 110 *livres* [99.99 pounds]. Its height demands skill and experience on the part of the grips who move it on the stage. Three men are enough. Two men set it on the mast and the other climbs up the mast ladder. He takes it [i.e., the wing] and fastens it with a small piece of rope called a "leader" after the other two have lifted it up to engage the bottom rail of the wing into the two iron hooks which hold it up a suitable distance from the stage floor. Only two men grip the wing, even if it is heavier; another man is no help. This part of the stage work is the most exhausting. I shall go into some details, because poor gripping can result in a wing falling, resulting in breakage of the joints or rails.

To grip a wing well, it should be held perfectly plumb. The two men who hold the sides should use the same hands, one as high as possible and the other "arm high." One man moves backwards and the other faces him. The first does nothing but lift the wing a little and if it tilts slightly out of plumb he can readjust it with his knee. The other always should keep his eye on the head of the wing to see that it is plumb and control it. The third is up on the ladder of the mast to detach or attach each wing.

It is the same for other types of flats, such as sloping ground rows, mountains and "inclinations," which lead to elevated places such as the rocks in the ballet of *Psyche.* All of these pieces are built on the stage floor where everything necessary for their construction is brought there.

The finished scenery for the next production as well as the hardware and accessories are stored in the side areas of the stage. Also, it is there that the actors, dancers, chorus, *corps de ballet* and supernumeraries await their entrances.

The entrances and exits of the different groups create unbelievable congestion, especially at the end of an act. It is after their exits, when the scene changes are made, that today's stages are very dangerous. Every day there is the risk of crippling someone because the space between the wings and walls is too narrow.

Chapter XIII

ON GRID MACHINES AND HOW TO
EQUIP A GLORY

A glory is the name given to a decoration composed of clouds which descends from the grid. It is composed of one or more decks and a group of clouds. At the great Salle des Spectacles in the Chateau of Versailles, I made a glory which had eight decks. Each one was fifty feet wide and five feet from front to back; they all descended from the grid. Naturally, many streets were used for this glory. When this ensemble of clouds carried sixty dancers onto the stage, the entire setting became a palace of Venus, and Venus herself descended from the grid in another group of clouds. This observation is made here so one will understand what can be done on a large stage which has a very strong grid and can support a considerable amount of weight.

An ordinary glory is made up of a deck, a back scene which can be on a flat or a dropcloth, a facing, and frequently one or more cloud clusters on either side. See Plate XI, *A*. The deck is usually thirty-six feet wide and three feet, three inches from front to back, since the streets on our stages are very narrow. On a large stage it is possible for the deck to be four feet, six inches from back to back. That is a good proportion, which makes streets easy to plan.

The deck is made of two heavy planks *B* which are set horizontally and joined together with enough cross-members *C* to maintain the spacing. So as to not affect the strength of the planks, the cross-members are not notched into them. Instead they are set in cleats which are attached above with bolts. It is completely covered with scantling.

When such a platform is flown, it is usually level. It is supported by four lines of brass rope *E*. These ropes should have thirty strands. Their lengths are determined by the height of the stage and the distance from their suspension points to the drum. With lines made of this material and of their gauge, it is possible to lift fifteen hundred *livres* [1,363.5 pounds] without worry, providing that they do not bind on themselves while turning.

The ends of these are attached with iron hooks to the corners of the deck. The other ends are run over to the motor drum and ordered there according to the gradient which is appropriate for the operation of the deck.

The drums which operate glories are in every way similar to those used below. They are rigged in the same way, using the same methods for the lines which run to the drums and the regulator, with this exception: Below, the regulator is always played out for raising or lowering. It is simply changed over at the drum. In the grid, it always remains on the same side of the drum.[56] One will ask why there is difference in this operation. To answer this question it is necessary to go into some details.

A glory or any other machine which descends from the grid must be raised back up again. Let us say that the four suspension lines have just been hooked up, and they are attached to the drum G.[57] For it to descend, it must first go up. The height to which it will be raised and the number of turns of the drum necessary to raise it to that height are known. The regulator L is wrapped around the gradient H of the drum in the opposite direction of the motor lines, and given an extra turn. When the machine redescends, it will be seen why this extra turn is prescribed. Then the counterweights which are intended to move it are raised with a winch to the proper height. Just as is done below, the counterweight line already has one end secured in the shackle of the counterweight. The other end is passed around the counterweight drum in the opposite direction of the motor lines. As the counterweight rises, responding to the movement of the winch, all the rigging is fed to the drum H and attached there. Therefore, it is certain and demonstrable that if the force of the weights is transferred to the counterweight line I, they will make the drum turn. However, it will turn much too fast. Therefore the counterweights need a regulator. Here is how to do it.

To move a glory, whose movement is up and down, a line is passed through the third sheave of the head block K, which runs, like the counterweight line, to the shackle of the counterweights where it is attached. This line is called the counterweight regulator. The other end is passed around the fixed roller in the corridor and tied off in the manner already indicated. Then the weights are released and the force is shifted to the counterweight line and the counterweight regulator. Here is the place to observe that there will always be three lines running through the blocks of the machinery in the grid: the winch line, the counterweight line, and the counterweight regulator.

These operations are completed, so let us follow the effect in this description.

By releasing the counterweight regulator, the weights lower. This heaves on the counterweight line, making the drum turn, and the glory ascends. The regulator feeds back on the turns it was given.[58] It is taken in very firmly around the fixed roller until the glory reaches it "out" position. Then this line is tied off on the cleat. If this line had not been given an extra turn, then, when the machine arrived to its "out" position, there would not be any line left around the drum, and one easily perceives that nothing would be restrained, neither the line nor the machine. Consequently, it is necessary that at least one extra turn or "tail" always remain on the drum for operating lines, motor lines, and glory lines. Otherwise one cannot be sure that they will hold.

The operation I just described completes the operation which we call "setting the glory in state." Now let us see what must be done to make the glory descend.

The counterweights have to be raised again, but if that is done, the machine will descend and it is not supposed to do that yet. What is to be done? This:

Since the regulator L is tied off at the cleat and wrapped around the drum in the opposite direction of the motor lines, it is quite impossible for the deck of the glory to descend. Let us continue with the operation.

The counterweights are raised with the winch. At the same time the counterweight line M is fed off the drum and carefully coiled up alongside it. The counterweight regulator is also fed back around the fixed roller and when the counterweight reaches its "out" position, the regulator is tied off to the cleat N.

The object of the first operation was to set the glory in state. The machine is too heavy to raise by hand, so the counterweights are used. This first operation does not actually count as a part of the actual operations but it had to be described.

Let us now suppose that the whistle has just been blown and see what happens. The regulator L is let out and the machine descends. While it descends, a machinist stationed at the counterweight drum M feeds the counterweight line from the coil back onto the drum. So it follows from this operation that the machine is lowered to the stage by the regulator while at the same time the counterweight line becomes taut again since it is fed back onto its drum.

When the counterweights are released by the counterweight regulator O, the glory reascends as a result, just as was the case in the first operation.

Great care should be taken to firmly withdraw the regulator L while the machine is ascending and this is why: If the counterweight regulator or the counterweight line should break, only this regulator would restrain the machine and keep it from falling. A fall would be a very great misfortune.

Glories are usually accompanied by clusters of clouds and they are always controlled by the same drum as the glories. Consequently, their movement is regulated by the same force. However, since different heights are predetermined for these clouds, each one travels a different distance, so their lines are attached to the appropriate gradient on the graduated drum. Drums of this nature are always called graduated drums. See Plate XIII.

Everything which flies in and out of the grid should be calculated to operate by the same methods and principles.

I should like to note that any grid machine which is very heavy, be it a glory or anything else, is counterbalanced by small counterweights called "lighteners." They are attached to the counterweight drum by lines which run in opposition to the motor lines, and their weight is calculated to set everything more or less in equilibrium. A lightener rises as the machine descends and it reduces the amount of weight necessary for the counterweight. Lighteners are also used in the operations which follow.

In one large movement during an opera in the Salle de Versailles, I used twenty-seven thousand weight[59] [24,543 pounds] of lighteners. One may judge for himself the counterweights used in the operation.

Chapter XIV

ON THE HIGH FLYING TRAVERSING MACHINES

These machines are not used any more, even though they can create many effects. However, since our stages are built as they are, great things are not possible. Furthermore, one cannot risk using it without exposing the suspension lines. This imperfection was tolerated in the past, but audiences today would find it unseemly. Our stages are too narrow, and it is necessary to have sufficient width on either side to control the maneuvers which are known as the marvels possible at the Opera.

As I describe the high flying traversing machine here, I feel obligated to communicate the means necessary to create it, and it can be used if finally opera, a native of France, should find asylum on the soil which gave it birth in a city whose commercial and industrial wealth could be dedicated to refined pursuits which prosperity makes indispensable. We have already given the name "Théâtre des Arts" to the genre.[60] Let us soon be able to stand in admiration of a building which may truly be a temple of the arts. My love for my art cries out for this vision, with all the passion possible from the heart of a Frenchman. So, I have departed a bit from my machines ... but I shall return to them.

A traversing machine is just like a glory. It is a deck with some sort of decoration, clouds, clusters of clouds, cars, etc., and it is also suspended by lines. Its effect is to pass across the stage while rising and lowering. The two latter movements are in common with a glory. See Chapter XIII.

Here is the operation which makes the machine move across the stage. Having determined the course it is to follow, a track is made whose supports A are attached to the joists of the main grid floor. See Plate XII, figure one.[61] On the conduits B an apparatus C, called the trolley, is set. The trolley should have sufficient play on the conduits so it can move easily from one side of the stage to the other. The trolley is equipped with four sheaves, two at each end. Two lines are enough for this machine. These lines are attached at one end to a drum, as is done for a glory which moves up and down. The other ends are passed through the set of two sheaves V which are seen centered on the support posts and then passed through the set of two sheaves *D,* which are located in either end of the trolley.[62] When the lines have been played out sufficiently, they are attached to the deck *E,* as is done for a glory.

On a sufficiently large stage, such a machine would have four lines. Then there would be two tracks, properly spaced.

Here is what one must do to keep the machine from rocking. The rope bridle *F* is attached to the deck *E,* and then it is attached to the lines by the ring *G.* Care should be taken that the ring be situated at least five feet above the deck of the machine. Since *G* is higher than the center of gravity, the whole apparatus may rock a little but it cannot turn over.

Having been rigged with its lines, the trolley is drawn across the track to the point *H.* Then a line is passed through the pulley *I* and attached to the hook *K* of the trolley and tied off at the cleat *L.* By releasing this line, the weight of the deck alone will naturally move the machine to the point *M,* following the dotted lines *NN.*

As was said before, the motor lines and the counterweight lines are rigged to their drums like those of a glory or a machine which moves up and down.

The trolley will cause the deck to descend to the point *M* as it moves along its track. To make the machine re-ascend to point *N* on the opposite side of the stage, do as follows: Take the line *R,* which is attached to the hook on the trolley *D,* and attach it to the shackle of the counterweight *P.* Then pass the other end of the line through the pulley *O* and securely fasten it to the counterweight *P.* Then attach a regulator, which is also by *R,* and tie it off to the cleat *S.* When this regulator is released, the machine will move to *M* via the dotted lines *NN* and re-ascend to *N* via the dotted lines *TT.*

If one wants a less circular path using a quarter less rise, here is what to do. (The drums are already rigged like a glory which moves up and down.) For the machine to pass across the stage in a more elliptical path and without rising very much, the motor lines are allowed to play out by releasing the regulator which is attached to the counterweight drum. This regulator is let out as much as necessary. By doing this, the deck will pass across the stage without rising very much from the path of its course line.

On the other hand, if one wants the machine to rise on a sharper than forty-five degrees, do the following: The motor drum is all ready to go. The full force of the counterweights is let fall on the counterweight regulator, and since this regulator and the counterweight line both run to the counterweight, the drum will turn as the regulator is let out and this will move the motor lines. Just as in the former operation, this operation is performed while the machine is in motion. There is great flexibility in this operation, depending upon the instructions which are given to the machinists who operate the drum regulator and the counterweight regulator. The machine may be made to rise to its full height, to whatever, depending on what is done with these two lines.

I reiterate, however, that these operations should only be performed on a large stage which is above all very wide. Otherwise the lines cannot be concealed. On a large stage, clouds are made to precede and follow the deck. They move in "love clusters" which mask the rigging from the eyes of the beholder, since seeing the rigging always destroys the illusion and the pleasure which it should give.

The same principles and methods govern the preparation and execution of the following operations so long as the stage is wide enough to accommodate them:

Traversing the stage at a single altitude, regardless of its height.

Traversing the stage while rising, either from the right or the left.

Traversing the stage while descending, either from the right or the left.

To do these things, one only has to return the trolley line one way or another.

It is also possible to use the two above methods of raising and lowering the car while it is moving to cause it to rise to the center of the stage and descend directly to the other side of the stage. This operation may be performed by beginning on either the right or the left of the stage.

It is easy to imagine the things that can be done with traversing machines wherever there is enough room to operate them. When one imagines a number of these machines set at different places and at different heights, presenting an ensemble of unified groups ingeniously and picturesquely displayed, one has an idea of the possibilities the opera has to create magnificent things; that is, when the creativity of the machinist is not restricted in his operations by the distressing construction of our theatres. Servadoni[63] never would have imagined that the techniques and operations created by his hardy hand would languish, nor would one of his genius have ever suspected that the art of creating and operating machines would be stifled in France by the lack of spacious stages.

This is just about everything necessary to say about the stage, its construction, and its machines. These details will be sufficient for those who are employed in its service and they should please those who want to know something about the methods used to create the scenes which amuse and interest them.

I highly esteem the art of the architect and I would not presume to give him lessons, reserving for myself a place of proper modesty.

Nevertheless, I feel that I should offer an observation here which might be very useful to those who profess an art which has created theatres in Paris and some of our principal cities. It might also be useful to those whose merit earns them the consignment of such great works.

All the buildings which the Romans consecrated for their pleasures were monuments. Ours, which have the same purpose, do not enjoy the same honors. Business interests determine most theatrical constructions for commercial profit, and their lack of good taste shows them to be what they are. The Romans had officials who supervised the erection of a building which was to be a public treasure, and where people gathered together in large groups to spend their leisure enjoying a fine theatrical production. We have seen companies buy land here and build theatres for their own purposes, but there was no such public authority overseeing their work or enforcing the necessary laws to provide for good exterior design and interior comfort. However, let us return to the limits of this essay and see where the architect and the machinist ought to plan and work together.

A theatre has the double objective of bringing together a large number of people and then creating a theatrical production for them to see, and the action on the stage is always what holds their attention. A newly decorated auditorium does not hold one's attention as long as a production on the stage, and the latter is what creates receipts at the box office. No one returns to a theatre a second time, no matter how beautiful the auditorium may be, if nothing is playing. Therefore it is necessary that the builder give much attention to the stage and sacrifice nothing to the auditorium; he should regard the latter as the last thing to occupy his thoughts. This observation is important also for those who are in charge of such constructions. If the architect, who wants to enrich his composition, and the machinist, whose ruler and compass might also be considered useful, are not brought into agreement, one is ruined before he even begins by an incommodious stage. If the proper arrangements are made, everything will be workable right from the beginning.

Chapter XV

ON THE SECURITY OF THE THEATRE, THE PLACEMENT OF THE PUMPS, RESERVOIRS, AND THE ROOM FOR THE FIRE BRIGADE

The wall which rises from the proscenium arch should extend ten feet above the roof to separate the grid from the attic over the auditorium. It is finished in practical gradients on either side and fitted with iron banisters to provide an easy access for the firemen and sufficient freedom for their operations in case of a fire. Another useful function of this wall is to stop fire from spreading from one attic to the other.

It is also good not to have any other access from the auditorium to the stage except the proscenium arch, which in a moment of danger of fire from the auditorium or stage can be closed with an iron curtain. This curtain should be constructed in the Odeon Theatre when it is built. I have given them the techniques and the plans. Both should be found in the Dewailly fire portfolio which regulated the work on that theatre.

However, an access between the stage and the auditorium is absolutely necessary. An opening of three feet by seven feet will do. The door is made of iron or bronze, and it is closed promptly after use.

The placement of the pumps requires the greatest of care. One needs a room for the fire brigade and a reservoir in the subterranean area of the theatre's basement. The firemen's room should be solidly vaulted and spacious enough for twelve men to operate a large pump which is always in good condition.

A squad of four firemen on duty at all times will always be prepared to go into action.

The reservoir, also vaulted, should be above or alongside the place occupied by the pump, but in such a way that the latter dominates the former, which will contain ninety *muids* [6,700 gallons] of water.[65] It should be serviceable in case of freezing by a good bridge made in place next to its two vaults. During heavy freezes, one should not rely on the usability of neighboring fonts whose reservoirs promptly freeze.

A special exterior stairway will lead the firemen and the pump operators to their room. The solidity of the vaults of this place and the certainty of exiting and entering without danger in case of fire will give confidence to the firemen, who will always be able to move in safety down to the last extremity.

Special reservoirs are necessary in the first and second floors beneath the stage. There is no danger except in the spaces of these two floors. At least twenty *muids* [1,489 gallons] of water will be maintained in each of them, which will be supplied by the large reservoirs of the stage and auditorium.

They will also be proportioned according to the need at the heads of the four service stairs of the stage. These will furnish, through crocks, the necessary water for the various high levels, for the dressing rooms, and to promptly arrest the progress of fire in the apartments and chimneys.

Later on I will show how, by dressing the wood everywhere possible, the number of combustible surfaces can be diminished.

In the placement and distribution of reservoirs I do not see how one can fail to design this essential: a reservoir to service the auditorium and cloak-rooms.

A guard corps of six soldiers on duty at all times will be maintained close by the theatre.

Chapter XVI

ON THE SERVICE FACILITIES FOR THE
STAGE AND THE PERFORMERS

All the stair landings which run to the level of the stage floor should be built without either a rise or a drop. Their construction should take into account the rake of the stage. This avoids tripping, which is especially dangerous for the dancers, as well as workers carrying loads.

There should be a dance studio very close to one side of the stage. It should be at least thirty-six by twenty feet, and the floor should be properly resilient.[66] Also, it should have the same rake as the stage floor, since it is here that the dancers practice and rehearse their dances. At the low end of the floor there should be a mirror in which the dancers can see themselves all the way down to their feet. There should be a large fireplace at the other end of the room. Another studio just like this one will be located on the other side of the stage. It will be just as close to the stage and it will provide the actor-singers a convenient place to await their entrances. It also will be used as a rehearsal hall. There should be at least fifteen dressing rooms on either side of the auditorium and they should be situated on different levels. The number at the Opera is not sufficient.

Two large rooms for dressing twenty young men and twenty young women are indispensable. They are located in the upper levels over the corridors in the grid of the stage house.

Two large rooms for the chorus, one for twenty-four men and the other for as many women, should be arranged on either side of the stage. They should be very nearby and located on a floor beneath the stage floor. Two large rooms for dressing one hundred fifty supernumeraries should be located at the back of the stage, and next to each one there should be a store-room for keeping the arms. All of these large rooms can be heated by stoves.

Two more rooms right next to the stage are absolutely indispensable. All the properties are stored there, such as flowers, garlands, spears, shields, quivers, bows, etc., etc.

While providing some understanding of the details involved with the facilities for the performers, I must also insist on providing them with everything possible for their ease and comfort. Their talents are the whole reason for having the theatre. Look to these details first and then to the object of this essay and then to my feelings for an institution to which I am very attached through long years of work which fortify the affection I have for it.

I shall end this chapter with two observations which may be useful:

1. It is possible to protect many things from fire by boarding over all the floors of the grid.
2. Nowadays when one has to be so thrifty with fuels of any kind, we should take advantage of some of the discoveries made over the last half a century. Provisions for heating have been far too neglected. The two methods of C.C. Desnarod and Mr. Bonnemain, both members of the Lyceum of Arts, should be very useful. Both can provide a solution to our problem, which is to find the best way to heat the stage, all the attendant areas, and every part of the auditorium and still reduce the tremendous amount of firewood necessary.

I have always thought that the two furnaces could be designed into the construction of the building. One should be in the well vaulted subterranean area of the stage and the other should be similarly located beneath the auditorium. They should be insulated so their heat is not lost, and the heat should be distributed by branching pipes fitted with valves to control the flow of heat. For example, the amount of heat sent to the auditorium could be varied in accordance with the size of the audience and large quantities of it could be redirected to the ducts beneath the stage. There it will rise and protect the lightly clad men and women from the discomforts of the cold. These people can be incapacitated by freezing temperatures.

The considerable smoke which arises from flaming properties requires a ventilator in the grid of the stage. Another one in the auditorium would also be useful but it should be ducted to the roof.

Chapter XVII

ON THE WAREHOUSES NEAR THE STAGE FOR STORING THE SCENERY

The necessity of a warehouse at least very near to the stage is recommended for many reasons. I shall enumerate a few of them:

1. Preserving the scenery, which breaks when it is moved roughly and when it is not carried perpendicularly,
2. Preserving the painting, which is effaced and damaged by chafing which results from transporting it too great a distance from the theatre,
3. The enormous expense of transportation and repairs to the painting, flats and drops. These two items alone cost the Opera more than 15,000 francs. Its warehouses on Rue Bergere are too far away from the theatre.

It would be better to build a warehouse for scenery close to the stage and at the same level, which would have the capacity of twenty complete settings, including wings, drops and borders. To move them easily from one to the other requires that the access be without unevenness or steps and that there be a door, closable with iron, which is thirty-one feet high, three feet wide at the bottom, and only eighteen inches wide at the top.

Chapter XVIII

ON THE AUDITORIUM, WHICH IS BOUNDED BY THE CURTAIN OF THE PROSCENIUM ARCH

I said previously that the opening of the proscenium, which determined all the dimensions of the stage, could also be used to give all the dimensions of the auditorium. Two reasons appear to demand that I return to this topic.

The first is the authority of Fontana,[67] and the second is my observations on a great number of theatres. At the end of my career, I can count many in France, Germany and Italy where I have made observations with the attentive eye of a stage builder, and I have built many theatres.

No auditorium appears to have been built according to any particular dimensions or definite outlines, except the Odeon, which has a fine plan. The diversity of plans shown by other auditoriums proves, therefore, that there is no one accepted theory and every theatre is simply built on its own.

I dare to speak in favor of such a theory here, and it appears to me that it applies to all theatres, large or small. See Plate IV, where I have given the outline of an auditorium, a parterre, and a proscenium.

If this is not the perfect form, it appears to me that it approaches perfection, since it gives the auditorium the advantage of being as long and high as it is wide. Furthermore, every seat provides the spectator with a good view of the stage as well as good audibility.

Determining the heights of the boxes is not just an arbitrary matter. The height of the first boxes, taken from the footlights of the stage to the rail of the stalls, should be five feet, six inches. The authority of the famous Lekain supports these observations.[68] He said that this height was the best for seeing and hearing well. The other rings of boxes are made in conformity with this one.

A space of twelve feet from the front of the first wing to the footlights is sufficient. The plan of the stage's apron is curved to allow the performers to step a little outside of the frame. The orchestra follows the same contour. Most importantly, this contour is the source of the illumination which emanates from the footlights contained therein. It is a good idea to seat the musicians on the "rays" which converge at the center where the maestro conducts. It should have a width of fifteen feet and be as long as necessary to accommodate the various musicians and their instruments. The floor is raked four inches per *toise* [two inches per yard] in the opposite direction of the rake of the stage, which banks the musicians, who should see and follow the actor on the stage, whether singing or dancing.

Between the front curtain and the first wing there should be a moving frame, situated to enlarge or diminish the opening of the proscenium. This frame or drapery should be very rich, since it frames the "moving tableaux" of the scene.

The curtain falls in front of it. Then the auditorium is left to itself, and terminated by the curtain.

Chapter XIX

ON THE BOXES IN THE AUDITORIUM

The fronts of all the rings of boxes should terminate flush, one over the other, a little short of the thickness which forms the proscenium arch, and not be set back one ring over the other, because this creates bad seats.

Each ring should be laid out so that its contour line in the circumference of the auditorium is recessed about two feet behind the contour line of the ring beneath it. This measurement is taken at the expense of the access corridors.

It is desirable that the floors of the boxes be raked and not level. Each one should have the same rake as the stage in the opposite direction. This is an advantage for the people seated in the last seats. This can be seen at the theatre of Porte St. Martin.

In the first boxes, four widely spaced rows of seats may be situated so that eight people may be comfortably seated in chairs. The last row may be railed off, if desired. Overall, they are superbly well situated seats.

The boxes of the second level may also accommodate four rows of seats, but the rows will be a little less deep than those of the first boxes in order to construct the levels which each row should have over the other. The last row may also be railed off.

Three graduated rows of benches in the third level of boxes will be sufficient to see and hear well.

The same applies to the fourth level, but it is necessary to increase the heights of the gradients a little more than those of the third.

The fifth level only has two rows on the sides. The center may be built as an amphitheatre which will seat at least three hundred people.

An auditorium should be resonant and it should not have any holes in any part of the ceiling, since these alter the sound, which destroys the public's primary pleasure, the ability to hear well. Neither should there be any boxes in the *voussoir.* It would be preferable to build a sixth level of boxes, leased by the year, close to which are installed all the necessary comforts and amenities, especially a stairway on each side where the tenants can come and go unseen.

In the spaces allotted for seating, the public seems to want comfortable accommodations. This is only fair, and they have been asking for this for a long time in return for their money. It is time they received it. They are not interested in seeing strange designs which are an annoyance, and the producers should understand just by looking at the box office receipts that anything which generates more traffic in the theatre is more profitable than static decorations.

One often encounters the question of whether or not to separate the boxes and create private accommodations for individual groups. This is not for me to say. However, in memory of the famous architect Peyre, I should note what European practice has deemed appropriate. Was it not a great pleasure to see two tableaux in the French Theatre, one on the stage and the other provided by the ladies who then had the right to present their beauty, grace and their finery of French taste within the frames of the boxes? One recalls these beautiful halls, which verify the truly appropriate words of Peyre, "An auditorium should be nothing more than a frame in which the tableau is brought to life by the ladies; no ornament, no shade of color should assume a character which might detract from the effects they desire to create." It is for everyone who feels this truth to come to its defense. The ladies should also lend their support.

Chapter XX

ON THE HALLWAYS LEADING TO THE BOXES

The hallways leading to the boxes should be sufficiently spacious, depending on their level. Those of the first and second ring should be wide and commodious, due to the traffic between the acts. Those of the upper rings may be smaller. However, all of them should terminate at the ends of the two sides of the theatre with landings whose stairs run from the top floor to the ground, and have a width of at least five feet. These dimensions take on a beautiful character in a fine monument. A hallway of the first or second ring which is not eight to nine feet wide will be cramped and uncomfortable, and the builder should be free to give it more space.

Chapter XXI

ON THE PARQUET OR PARTERRE AND ORCHESTRA

The methods used today of fixing the seats to the parterre do not
allow it to be elevated to the level of the stage floor for balls. For the
convenience of the public, the parterre should be raked in gradients
toward the stage, three inches per *toise* [one half inch per foot] or
three inches per row of seats. One enters through two doors, as near
as possible to the high end of the hall, so that the latecomers do not
disturb those who have already arrived when they seat themselves.
Two other doors, quite near to the orchestra, and always ready to
open, are indispensable. They are opened at the end of the performance.

The orchestra is at the end of the parterre and it has a sufficient
rake of its own. Five benches with backs are set in it, and one enters
by two doors, one on each side.

Chapter XXII

ON THE FOYERS AND OTHER FACILITIES NECESSARY FOR THE CONVENIENCE OF THE PUBLIC

Two foyers will be provided, one on the level of the first boxes and the other on that of the third. The first one should be richly decorated and furnished with mirrors. It can be used for rehearsals if the theatre does not have a stage for that purpose, and it can also be used for dance.

The second foyer, on the level of the third boxes, may be smaller, and if the theatre has such a foyer, it is preferable for rehearsals. In this case, the first foyer should only be accessible via the offices.

Stoves will be provided in the soundest fashion, with great attention given to the prevention of fires in the vestibules, stairs and foyers. In the latter locations, there should be independent chimneys for the stoves at either end.

Cold and humidity should be shut out as much as possible for the drums and heavily loaded battens.

I repeat my view here, for the construction of vaulted-over furnaces in the two basements. This would result in great economy, better distributed heat and less danger.

The paying public, whose money supports the performances, has a right to consideration. Precautions should be taken to insure safety and comfort when they arrive. Both are found in very large vestibules.

The first, an enclosed vestibule, will be closed in the winter by doors paned with glass, and it should be able to hold a large number of people who may move about easily without bumping into each other as they go to the ticket windows.

The second vestibule is in the interior and at the foot of the grand staircase. It should be as large as the former, very bright, providing a sparkling atmosphere, and furnished with comfortable seats for the ladies in a temperature which allows them to wait warmly for their carriages. Since he creates the decor, the builder will without doubt make it rewarding to a sex for whom this "second performance" should be pleasant since they provide the adornment.

Chapter XXIII

SOME DETAILS ON THE INTERIOR OF THE
AUDITORIUM AND THE STAGE

There are many theories on ways to provide the orchestra with all
the sonority it needs, and many things have been tried.

Experience shows that the inverted vault in stone or brickwork
advocated by some people to accommodate the orchestra is a poor
solution and should be rejected. One was built of stone in the large
theatre at Versailles, and far from projecting sound, it absorbed it. It
had to be torn out and rebuilt in wood. The one that Soufflout had
built in the theatre at the Tuileries did not do a thing, and it would
not hold all of the musicians. At the Palais Royal, Moreau was no
more satisfied with this system than the others, and all the musicians would not fit into the vault.

It was by chance that a poorly laid-out floor which supports the
orchestra at the Opera was not unfavorable to the sounds of the instruments. Here is my opinion on this very important part of an opera house:

A foundation of masonry laid on the ground supports a stone dias
and beams are laid on top of this. Strong joists are set on these and
very dry fir planks which are tongued and grooved will be set firmly
over these joists. I have indicated a masonry foundation because one
may presume that an instrument (and that is what an orchestra is)
would be muted if it were attached to the ground.

The front of the stage also requires care in producing good sound.
It is an essential part of the orchestra.

Across the entire curve of the front of the stage, which is walled in
brick, very dry strong fir planks are well joined and affixed perpendicularly. This method creates good audibility in the auditorium for
those who make the sound. It was used when the large theatre at
Versailles was reconstructed and it worked well.

There is another thing, the comfort of the musicians. They do not
like being cramped one on top of another, and as they say, "playing in
their neighbor's pocket."

The basement of the parterre should be sealed to prevent the passage of air and cold.

The dividers of the boxes should not be made of light wood nor their bases of wooden panels, because of the many openings. They are not lathed. They are covered over with many nails with heads, which receive and hold the plaster well. The interior is dressed in light, well joined wood. This construction makes the hall very sonorous. It worked perfectly at the large theatre of Versailles.

The corridors of the boxes require a tiled floor and plastered ceilings to avoid the seepage of water spilled by negligence and impropriety in the floor above.

For the same reasons, one may decide to tile and plaster the floors and ceilings of the stalls. Also, consider the necessity of giving fire as little fuel as possible. This consideration also determines the use of plaster for the vaults, cornices, and all the surfaces to which it may be applied.

An opera house should hold around three thousand five hundred people on big days or sell-outs, and give a very full appearance with less than twenty-four hundred. This is because an empty house bores the spectator and discourages the performer.

It seems to be proven that blue patterned wallpaper, or chocolate, do not fatigue the vision and are very much favored by the ladies. Much can be said to support blue boxes, a color which is becoming to their hands.

Too many ornaments, figures, masks and grotesqueries are not attractive on the fronts of the boxes. Some arabesques in good taste and on a ground pleasing to the eye (and I repeat, most of all to the ladies) appear to please all tastes that have been formed after twenty years of our modern theatres.

The ceiling will be more disposed to receive all the embellishments which require a round shape. It is for this ceiling that the above dimensions are indicated.

However, in creating the interior decor of the hall, it should be remembered that smoking makes it necessary to repaint about every seven or eight years, and to do it very well can become very expensive; one should not let this happen.

I think I should say that it is a necessity as well as a nicety to reserve the two center boxes. One should be reserved for the painter-decorator[69] and the machinist, and the other for the author, lyricist and composer. There they will see the effects of their work and in receiving the impressions of the public they will better make corrections and additions.

All of these arrangements are deemed essential in Italy. There, everything pays homage to art. Here, one sacrifices to the interest of the businessmen. In fact, who has not seen authors and composers arriving late in the hallways of the Opera because they are frugal with their time, wandering about frantically looking for a way to elbow their way into the opening of some box? This is a fine reward for those who dedicate their evenings to the public's enjoyment and fat profits in the box office. The *ecu* it costs for the seat reserved for the author could bring a thousand in return.

If I enter into details which overlap those which are in the domain of the builder, I do so for three reasons: the habit of observing what works best in every part of the theatre, the certainty of pleasing the public, who for a long time have desired most of the things I have indicated, and the obligation to point out those things necessary for the health and comfort of the singers and dancers.

I do not pretend to set the difficult art of the machinist above its legitimate place, but I believe that I have demonstrated that an architect who builds a theatre and prepares all the initial work to be done, which is very expensive, without consulting the machinist, builds problems into the theatre which will always interfere with the operations.

It is much better to work together than to be far away from the machinist and do something poorly which will always be interfering with something else, force you to spend much, and never work properly.

Chapter XXIV

ON THE METHOD OF LIGHTING THE AUDITORIUM
WITHOUT DETRACTING TOO MUCH FROM
THE EFFECTS ON THE STAGE

In Italy there are no lights in the auditorium during the performance. In France, on the contrary, and especially in Paris, there is illumination. It can be a nice effect to see and be seen, but it is accomplished at the expense of what is taking place on the stage.

A middle course should be considered. The chandelier can be lighted with as many lights as desired, and lowered to the level of the second stalls. When the overture begins, or better still, when the curtain goes up, it is raised up to the ceiling. Placed under a bell of light blue gauze, it will spread a sweet and equal illumination to all parts of the auditorium. The effects on the stage will be preserved. During intermissions, it is released from the gauze and, descending to its place, it will shed its brightness.

The bell can also be lowered, but the operation can be very troublesome, since it may slip on the brass rope. Thus an alternative is found so that the stage and the auditorium may be lighted.

With today's method, sanctified by habit, the chandelier destroys all the night and dusk effects, and all the tints of lighting prescribed for the illusion.

The distribution of light between the wings, borders and drops is always under the control of the decorator,[70] who decides for himself how they should be arranged according to the subject of the work. Thus the stage should be lighted with intelligence and in conformity with the scenery which it brings into view.

Chapter XXV

ON THE METHOD OF HEATING
THE STAGE WITH STOVES

Though I felt obliged to expound in a previous chapter on the desire to see a stage heated with subterranean furnaces whose heat would be better and cheaper to distribute, I should not silently neglect the method of arranging the stoves in this important part of the theatre.

The rigors of winter are cruel to the performers on a large stage. It is necessary then to provide everything possible to make it less painful and to guarantee that they will not be unable to perform, or catch cold, which makes the box office languish during the season because of their absence. Therefore, let us give them the warmth that they do not get from clothing.

The fear of fire is the basis for not putting stoves on the stage, but just because that is a very important consideration, does that mean that we cannot conceive of ways to do it safely? In the places which I shall design, the stoves will be set on pedestals in fairly large lead basins which are kept filled with water. This first precaution is easy to appreciate. They are used in gun-powder mills. I used them for two winters at the Feydeau Theatre without accident. Cast iron stoves are preferable. They generate and give off the best heat. Their smoke pipes should be of strong sheet iron to resist shocks. One on each side of the stage in the corners behind the proscenium, at stage level, will be convenient for the performers to warm their feet in front of a grill a few inches from the opening. The smoke pipes of these stoves will carry the heat to reservoirs found in the grid corridors.

Beneath the stage near to the seventh plan or street, a heat reservoir will be provided on either side at the level of the street, because operations are very cramped here.

Two [stoves] are located in each up stage corner at stage level, and they dispose of their excess heat via the pipes into reservoirs which radiate their heat into the grid corridors.

One stove will provide heat in each staircase by zigzagging the stovepipe.

Tightly closing the revolving doors to the outside, the windows, the ventilating windows in the basement, and a ceiling in the grid will assure an adequate heat in the theatre. After the performance, the prompt and careful closing of the exits will not permit the cold to re-enter.

Chapter XXVI

ON THE DANGERS OF FIRE AND HOW
TO PROTECT A THEATRE

I have seen many theatres burn. None of them were the victims of fires started during a performance. At that time, so many eyes are open everywhere that it is inconceivable that at the Opera, for example, there should be any fear on the part of the spectators. They know that they are surrounded by surveillance, precaution, full reservoirs, pumps in good order with their intelligent operators always on the job. All this should inspire the public with the most perfect security. Two opera houses and the Odeon burned down before my eyes and none burned during a performance. It is not a bad idea to examine the causes.

The first burned through the carelessness and stupidity of a sweeper who set his candle on the act curtain counterweight in the substage area and then went away and left it there. The flame set the new ropes on fire. The curtain burst into flame and the fire spread. I was wounded.

The second was destroyed in nearly the same way. A burning curtain cannot be separated from its lines at both ends at the same time. It remained hanging and burning and the fire spread to the dropcloths in the grid. The fire could have been put out if the means to do so had been at hand. The reservoirs were full but there were neither pumps nor firemen in the theatre. Help was more than an hour in coming. I was wounded again.

The Odeon burned at seven in the morning. I arrived before eight. The fire had not developed to its full force, but I could see it burning violently in three parts of the theatre, in the back of the stage, house left and to the left in the back of the auditorium. The origins of the fire seemed to be scattered.

None of these fires took place during a performance.

After the fire at the Palais Royal I suggested the means to create security through careful precautions. Some of them were adopted.

In the year 4,[71] the Feydeau Theatre survived only because it was completely sealed. There were no drafts of air to spread the fire which had started.

The burning of the little Théâtre des Elèves on the Boulevard finally forced more attention to be directed to these accidents.

I noted in a *memoire* the means to extinguish fires in theatres, and above all the ways to prevent them. I mentioned the necessity of a paid fire brigade and of always having men available to man the pumps and firemen to operate the hoses. Nowadays a round-the-clock guard is maintained at the Opera. These wise measures were adopted recently by order of the government. To perfect these measures, the firemen and guardsmen should be combined every night. A machinist from each of the three parts of the stage will also be with them. One who knows the grid, one the stage, and one the substage area can be helpful because they know how to perform any of the operations in these areas well, due to the nature of their work.

Neither a guardsman nor a fireman knows the positions of the flying bridges as well as a machinist and they move clumsily and less quickly.

Of all the precautions taken at the Opera, there is one which has been publicized that contributes quite a bit to public safety, and that is the one which is employed when flaming properties are used on the stage.

Everywhere, close at hand, there are buckets full of water in which there are large sponges. Wherever a fire might start, it is quickly extinguished.

However, to stop the spread of devastating fires, here are some additional methods which I believe are useful, since long experience has taught me so.

Fire has no effect on wood covered with an inch of plaster. Having seen three theatre fires, I noticed that the jambs of stone were reduced to chalk and the lintels remained intact, preserved in plaster. They had been put to the test, and the most intense fire did not burn them.

The surface of all wood capable of taking plaster could be plastered without interfering with the operation or movement of the machines.

Fire does not act quickly on dropcloths which are painted on both sides. They burn slowly and without flame. The hemp fabric is painted with an earthen substance on its two surfaces and fire can only work slowly on the combustible material in between them. It is not necessary to observe that oil is not used as a base when painting dropcloths for the stage.

I could not let that observation pass by. I want to see us use every means possible to discourage fires in theatres.

All dropcloths are sized at first with a glue size in which very fine, sifted plaster is diluted.

For a number of years, wool has been proposed as a material for dropcloths because it makes no flame when burning. The scene painter will encounter great difficulty painting on woolen cloth unless the methods of manufacturing it are perfected so that the brush behaves the same as it does on hemp.

While we are waiting for new discoveries which will make spun and woven wool useful for the stage, I think we can use the method I just described and make our scenery less combustible.

I shall finish this essay with a chapter in which I give the details of how to mount a theatrical production, which I noted in one of the earlier chapters.

ON THE NECESSITY OF GIVING THE STAGE A VERY LARGE WIDTH FROM ONE LATERAL WALL TO THE OTHER, FOR THE EASE OF CONVENIENTLY MOUNTING THE SCENERY FOR A PRODUCTION WHICH IS EXECUTED IN VERY LARGE SPACES

To set the stage[72] one must:

1. Mark out the plans or streets where the different pieces of scenery, dropcloths, ceilings, friezes, cupolas, skies, etc. must be,
2. Designate the streets which carry scenery and those which do not,
3. Finally, calculate the points where the wings stop when they run on stage, whether it be for an act or a whole opera or ballet.

All of this cannot be done unless one calculates the number and type of pieces needed, the places they occupy relative to what they will represent, and the different between the spaces in a public place, a field, a palace, a temple, an apartment or a prison.

I should remark here that one of the most striking effects of the stage is one which surprises the spectator by changing quickly from a small place to a large one, from a palace to a prison, from a pleasant field to a desert, and in effect to present him with contrasts. He does not understand the difficulties which have to be overcome to interest and please him, but he enjoys the surprises contrived for him and he applauds variety, rapid scene changes, and the machinist is rewarded for his labors.

In order to clarify the development of the three principles I have just presented, I shall assume that I have to mount the sets for the opera *Hecuba*.

The first is a public place.

The second is the main part of a huge palace.

The third is the interior of the Temple of Apollo.

The fourth is a private and secluded part of the Palace of Priam, dedicated to his gods, the Penates.

The fifth is the city of Troy after it has been burned.

The first of these settings should occupy the whole stage. It should offer a perspective of great buildings, temples, a palace, monuments, and provide large entrances and exits. In effect, it is a place of vast expanse where many people assemble.

It is easy to see that in order to do such settings there must be a very large, very wide stage. Depth is necessary, without doubt, but it is less essential than the dimensions laid out in the preceding chapters because depth is represented on the dropcloths with the techniques available to the art of perspective.

However real space is needed in the width. First, without it the side walls of the stage are visible during scene changes. Second, enough space is required off stage of the wings on either side for all the people necessary for the scene and their number should not interfere with the machinist's work.

One says "shift the scenes"[73] in the theatre, and not "make them move," or "make such and such a wing appear in such and such streets." I shall explain.

Let us suppose that a palace occupies the first four or five plans on one side of the stage in the public place of *Hecuba*, and that one wants it to be on the corner of a large street.[74] If that street is depicted on the fifth or sixth plan, too small a part of it will be seen, but if one shifts to the seventh or eighth, the space enlarges on the stage and so it appears to the eye of the spectator. The perspective[75] unites the space, offering him a street or an immense space.

The advantage of this arrangement is that a troupe of armed soldiers, a crowd, or a number of people can comfortably make their entrances without having to enter through walls,[76] [as is the case] when the setting is poorly laid out with one part here, protruding into another street, and one there, running into another.

This method of shifting scenery is ordinarily done from the right or left, to such and such point, depending on the demands of the setting.

This is the place to comment on the great amount of co-operation necessary between the machinist and the painter-decorator.[77] The machinist first reads a poem or ballet and grasps the intentions of the author. Then he draws up his plan of the schedules to be made for the machines to move, and he calculates which machines will carry which decorations while determining with the painter[78] which wings should work with them and all the scenery for the production.

Let us return to *Hecuba*. The first set should occupy all the space the stage has to offer.

The second, which is the main part of the palace of Priam, should only occupy seven streets. Terminating it at this point facilitates the clearing of what was on stage in the first scene and the setting up of what will be the back of the temple.

This temple, the third set, can extend to the ninth street. Like the public place, it is amenable to grand effects. In order to achieve this, the settings must be shifted according to the demands of its architectural composition.

The fourth setting is the part of the palace of Priam consecrated to the Penates. It necessarily has less space than the previous settings. It needs fewer exits. Its composition and the period of time it is in place make it possible to clear everything that was the temple and set up everything which will represent a part of Troy, the fifth and last set of *Hecuba*. For this one, it is impossible to have too much space, either in width, depth, or height. The burning of the town cannot be well executed except in a large area where the operations are not constrained. The operations should not encounter any obstacles at all.

I chose *Hecuba* for an example because nothing should be small in a town where the walls were built by Neptune and the temples by Apollo.

This opera demanded much effort and one could appreciate the effects, but I dare say that they would have been much more effective on a stage whose size was commensurate to the grandeur of the subject. No one knows how many fine and supernatural stage illusions can be created by giving the machinist and the decorator[79] the opportunity to ply their art on a stage large enough to permit the marvelous and the grand which make up opera.

I should not fear reproach for repeating a little on the necessity of a very large stage, because the lack thereof is detrimental to all the backstage work, operations, singing, dancing, the chorus, the *corps de ballet* and the supernumeraries. The example of shifting scenery in *Hecuba* is the proof, and any other work could provide it also.

I say that if there is only a narrow and distressing space on either side of the great frame which encompasses the sets, where in laying out the effects the sets have to be shifted, where is it possible to put the multitude of people demanded by a large production?

One may recall again that the last act of *Alceste* where, right and left, the layout of the scenery required wings to move in the many streets and one could never see the workers, singers, dancers or supernumeraries in the wings.

We come around the back of the present stage but it is not [done] without innumerable problems or risking the lives of many people.

I should observe on this subject that this daily inconvenience in narrow spaces is detrimental to the financial interests of the Opera.

The costumes get crumpled, dirtied and torn. The embroideries are spoiled, the muslins, gauzes, flowers and garlands of the dancers lose their freshness in the press of the pushing, crowding multitude. A costume does not last as long as it would if those who wear them could go easily and without constraint to any place their roles call them.

But one of the strongest considerations for having a stage of great width is the necessity of having the settings of the repertory close at hand, especially when a large warehouse is not right next to the theatre.

In the old days, the machinist hardly knew the word "repertory." A production was mounted and it played for three months in a row.

Today, the productions vary at the Opera, as at other places. The settings must always be ready. Often, even the Opera has been brought to a halt by an emergency. The administration could only give a late notice that the arrangements on the stage had to be changed. There is no time to lose in cartage if the warehouses are far from the theatre. All the settings for whatever productions possible, are necessarily stored in the lateral areas of the stage.

The desire to concur promptly with the administration of the Opera to execute ways to vary the pleasures of the public makes it a law for the machinist to do what might be called a *tour de force* on the present stage which has not been properly built with the basic constructions necessary for the kinds of productions which are given there.

A few details are indispensable here for the satisfaction of the spectators who will no longer be led into misunderstanding the correct movement of scenery and machines after they know that the spaces are not proportionate to the multitude of objects which are brought into their view in the course of a production where it is necessary to make the eleven changes, for example, in the three acts of an opera or ballet.

From one street to another, there is a given space. It should be the same above in the grid; that is to say, those spaces where the ceilings, the dropcloths, and the skies are suspended and should descend between one wing and another. But this is not so. This stage was not planned to execute the *tour de force* or to set up and shift eleven changes. The set of friezes is such that the dropcloths are not hung perpendicular to the space between each wing. They can only fall way behind so they must be guided. Before the whistle is blown, machinists are perched on the bridges of each side, ready to guide the borders into the spaces between the wings by preventing them from falling on their own line of descent, which is away from the space, and they do not create the effect they are supposed to produce. This operation is performed inside, the minute counterweight is released.

So should one be surprised at a mistake in the shift? In spite of the swiftness of the corrective measures employed by foreseeing and rendering them impossible, one is not always quick enough to wing the indulgence of the audience, which is the only incentive for me to endure the pains I take to please them and give me renewed energy to merit their indulgence. I pray that one is convinced that a false stop which can occur in a shift makes me doubly chagrined to be cramped in a narrow stage, and that whoever agrees with my discontent will unite his desires with mine so that finally popular demand for an opera house will cause one to be built which is worthy of the love the French have for the Theatre, and of the rightful admiration of foreigners.

END OF ESSAY

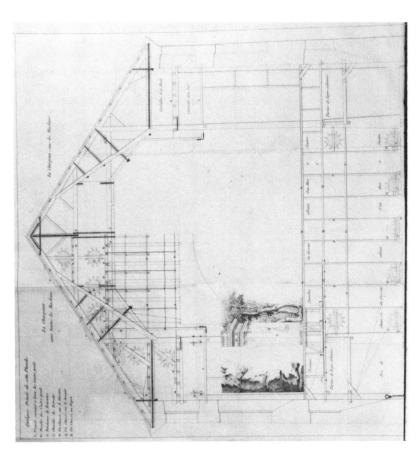

Plate I Front Elevation of a Stage

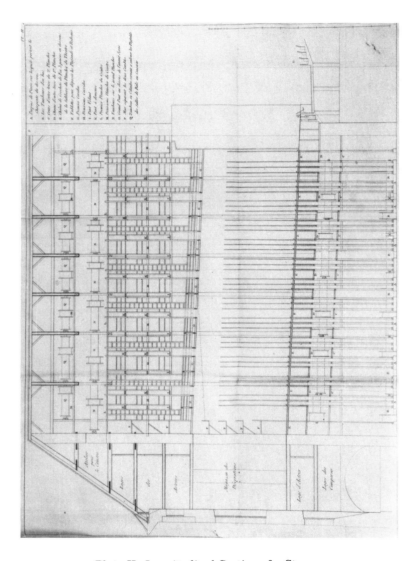

Plate II   Longitudinal Section of a Stage

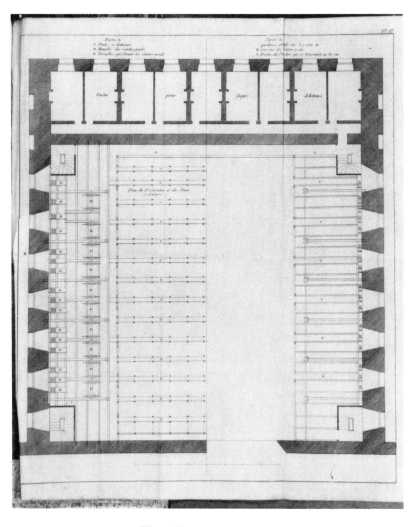

Plate III   Plan of the Grid

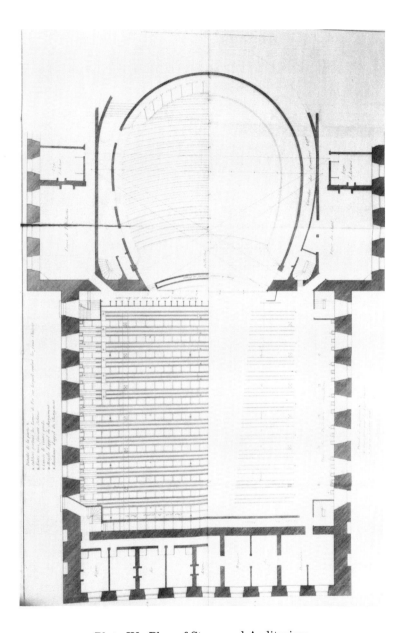

Plate IV   Plan of Stage and Auditorium

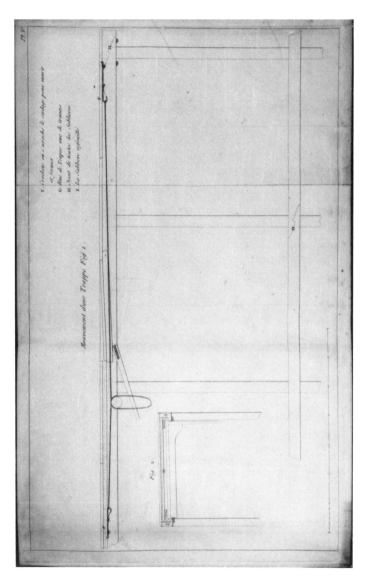

Plate V Mechanism for Operating Sliding Trap Doors

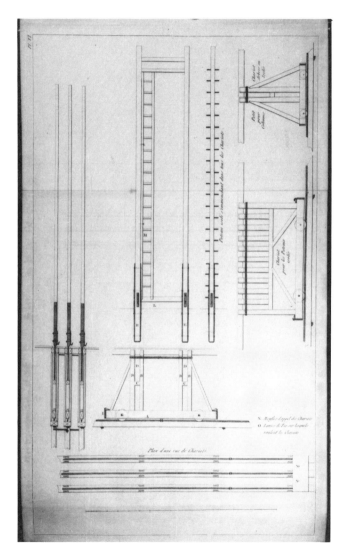

Plate VI   Designs for Chariots and Chariot Tracks

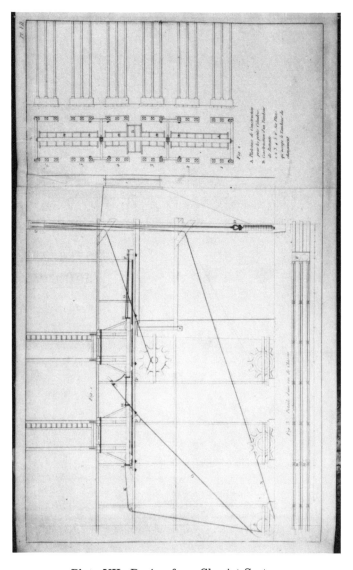

Plate VII Design for a Chariot System

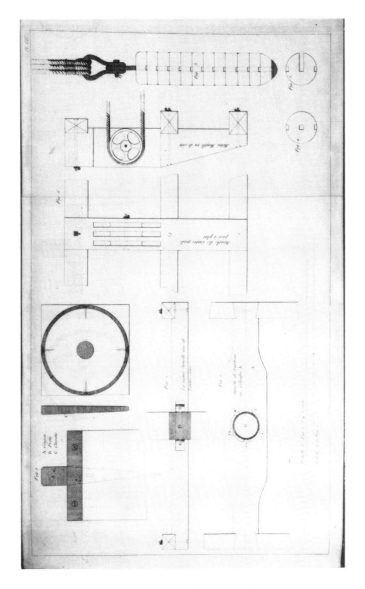

Plate VIII Machine Details

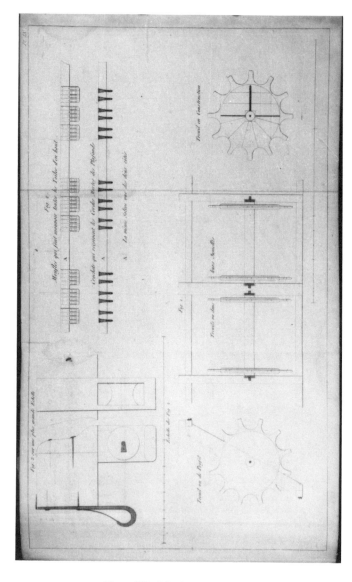

Plate IX   Machine Details

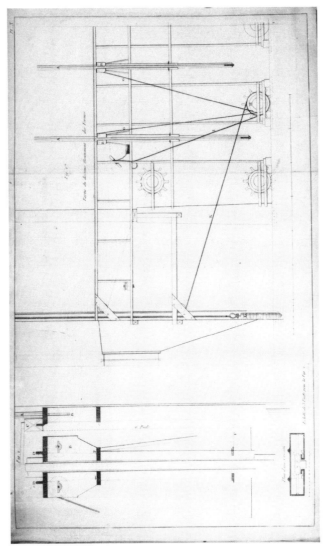

Plate X   Cassettes Rigged on the Stage and Cassette Details

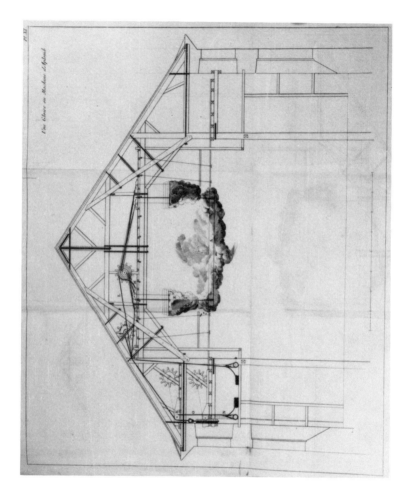

Plate XI   Design for a Glory

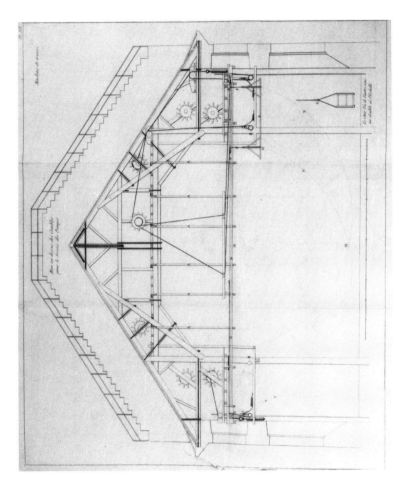

Plate XII Design for a Horizontal Flying Machine

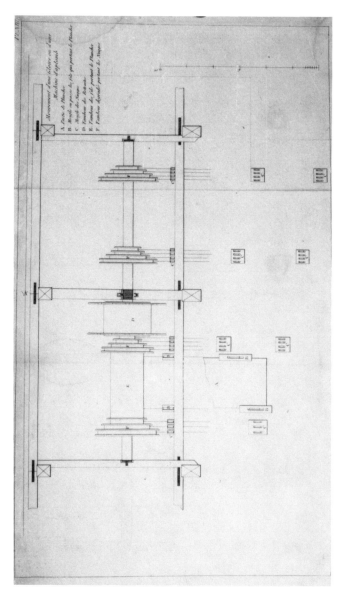

Plate XIII   Design of a Motor for a Glory

Footnotes

[1]April 4, 1801. Boullet uses the revolutionary calendar of the First Republic.

[2]French, *spectacle.*

[3]February 19, 1801.

[4]1799.

[5]The fronts and partitions of the boxes as well as the entrances, the proscenium arch and the Royal Box were usually decorated with lavish designs in relief and paint. As these designs were often allegorical, Boullet calls them *elogés* or eulogies, which has been translated here as "motif." Later Boullet refers to their having been extravagant or overly done. His complaint here is that theatre builders were more concerned with auditorium decor than with the technical considerations of the stage.

[6]Marie-Joseph Peyre, 1730-1785, is known to have introduced new architectural concepts based directly on classical concepts. He and Charles de Wailly, 1729-1798, built the Théâtre de l'Odeon.

[7]French, ". . . trop tôt enlevé aux arts . . ." That is, he died too soon.

[8]*Boullet's footnote:* "Peyre is responsible for the project for an opera house whose well executed model has been stored for a long time in the room which precedes the large theatre at the Versailles Chateau. Peyre created the building for the Comedie Française on the land of the old Condé Hotel. It would have been three arcades wider and five longer if the original plans had not been changed by some meagre visioned people. Good taste desired a temple dedicated to Melpomene and Thalia to be erected in the St. Germain district. It is bereft today of their presence." Note: At this time, the Comedie Française was housed in the Théâtre de l'Odeon and St. Germain was the most prestigious district in Paris.

[9]Arnout, also spelled Arnould and Arnout, was the *Machinist du Roi* from 1747 till approximately 1757 when his name becomes obscured by Girault.

[10]*Opera du Paris.* Boullet consistently refers to the Paris Opera as simply "the Opera." When he wrote this work the Paris Opera was housed at the Théâtre des Arts.

[11]French, *pieds*. The *pied* is equal to one English foot.

[12]The distance from the stage floor to the grid is twice the height of the proscenium arch.

[13]French, ". . . *la ligne perpendiculaire de la plate-bande* . . ." In American stage design, this is called the "plaster line."

[14]I.e., *designer's elevation.*

[15]French, *ceintre*. This word has no equivalent in modern American theatre terminology. Its equivalent in architectural terminology is "attic." Here it refers to the entire area above the stage floor, including the corridors, first and second machine floors, etc. It has been translated simply as "grid" although the stage Boullet is discussing actually has two grid floors.

[16]French, *decorateur*. Though *decorateur* can be translated as "designer" in modern French, there is no indication in this work that anything resembling a designer in the modern sense is meant. Indeed, Boullet makes the secondary role of the *decorateur* very clear in chapter XXVII when he shows that the machinist, not the *decorateur* made the major design decisions in the planning of a production. Elsewhere in this work, Boullet uses the term *peintre-decorateur*, [painter-decorator], and sometimes just *peintre*, [painter], to refer to the same person. It is clear that the role of designer, as thought of today, is not meant by Boullet.

[17]Till Voltaire stopped the practice, benches were provided on the stage itself, just inside the proscenium arch on either side, and spectators who were willing to pay the extra price could sit there. Boullet is referring to these fashionable spectators as *merveilleux*, or "dandies."

[18]The back wall includes the roof peak.

[19]The side walls are tied together by the joists in the grid floors and the tie beams.

[20]French, *toile*. *Toile* is a general term which refers to any hanging cloth scenery, including painted drops. American stage terminology sometimes uses the term "soft scenery" to mean the same thing. Thus, the term has been consistently translated as "dropcloth" and occasionally "drop" when the context makes it clear that other soft scenery is not in question. As Boullet also uses the specific terms, *bandes d'air* [sky borders] and *plafondes* [ceiling borders] when referring to borders, meaning is usually clear except when he uses *toile* in the general sense such as in this sentence. Consequently, "dropcloth" should usually be interpreted in the general sense of "soft scenery."

[21]A street is the horizontal space which lies between one order of wings and the next. In the broader sense, it includes on order of wings as well. "Plan" is a synonym for street.

[22]A mast is a removable portion of the chariot which protrudes up through the chariot slots in the stage.

[23]Boullet is prescribing the location of the rafters in the grid in relation to the chariots on the stage. See Plate 8.

[24]The shocks Boullet refers to are the vibrations and stresses made by the large number of machines which were used in the stage house simultaneously to change the scenes and create spectacular effects.

[25]Boullet gives no weight reference here, which is probably a typographical error. However, since he consistently uses the Paris *livre* elsewhere in this work, it is assumed that he meant to use it here. The Paris *livre* was equal to 0.909 English pounds.

[26]French, *mi-plats.*

[27]French, *pouce.*

[28]French, *sapin.*

[29]Boullet gives small measurements in the Paris *ligne,* which was equal to one-twelfth of an inch. Consequently, measurements such as five-sixths of an inch are not uncommon in this work.

[30]French, *toiles.*

[31]These containers were probably similar to carriage lamps of same time in which a candle was inserted into a tube fitted with a spring. The candle compressed the spring and a threaded grommet or bezel was screwed on the top of the tube to keep the candle compressed inside the tube. As the candle burned away, the spring forced the candle up, level with the grommet.

[32]French, *faux cordages.* I.e., trim lines.

[33]The term, "grand drape," refers to teasers and tormentors in this case. This is not the same as modern American usage in which the grand drape is only the front teaser.

[34]I.e., the lower corridors.

[35]*Boullet's footnote:* "It is not recommended to use the kind of fir which comes from Vosges for the construction of this floor. The hard ligneous portion of its grain causes grooves to form, since it is so hard and not affected by friction as the softer portion is. This results in the floor becoming uneven and, in some places, slippery, which is dangerous for the dancers. The fir from Auvergne should be used instead. It is even-grained, more flexible, softer, and almost totally uniform in soft fiber. It is possible to have it delivered in Paris at no great expense. It can be loaded on a ship on the Allier River at Pond-du-Chateâu. It would arrive here via the Loire and our canals of the Orléanais. It appears to me that ballet demands the use of this particular fir. The more perfect one becomes, the more difficult things he attempts. The machinist must provide every possible means for the execution of such things in ballet and reduce the danger of slipping on some

part of the wooden floor which have become slippery due to constant friction."

[36]The notch deepens as it runs off stage.

[37]Timbers were not finished on all four sides as they are now.

[38]A piece of strap iron is set on edge in this groove to create the track.

[39]Boullet is actually describing a large system of hooks and eyes which join all the support posts in the substage area.

[40]Boullet uses the term *faux chassis* or "false wing" when referring to a mast.

[41]French, *cuivre*. *Cuivre* means "copper" in modern French and the only mention of the modern term *laiton* [brass] in the entire work is the single reference to brass rope in Chapter XIII. However, in older French usage, *cuivre* could be ambiguous since *cuivre rouge* [red copper] meant "copper" while *cuivre jaune* [yellow copper] meant brass. As copper is a very soft metal which would soon wear out if used for the equipment Boullet describes, *cuivre* has consistently been translated as "brass" in this work.

[42]The masts would diminish in height, order per order up stage, when perspective scenery was used. Boullet does not show this arrangement in his Plate II.

[43]In the following discussion Boullet uses the term *arbre*, translated as "axle" in the dual sense of both axle and drum. This is because, as he explains later, the drums were built around the axles after they had been installed in their places.

[44]French, *changement.*

[45]French, *chene de brin*. Boullet apparently means that each axle should be made from a single tree trunk with the heart wood in the center, as opposed to cutting sections from a larger piece.

[46]An "X" is drawn from corner to corner on the end of the axle to establish its center.

[47]There are sometimes two and sometimes three lines attached to the counterweight drum depending on whether the hand operated regulator is attached to the drum or directly to the counterweight. Boullet confuses the issue here because his distinction between the counterweight line, the regulator, and the winch line is not clear. His final reference is actually to the winch line.

[48]The term, counterweight drum line, *retrait au tambour,* could actually refer to any of the lines attached to the counterweight drum: the regulator, the counterweight line or the winch line.

[49]*Lignum vitae.*

[50]The label *B* is missing from this plate. The reference is to the winch just under the chariot on the right.

[51]French, *deux mille pesant. Livres* is assumed.

[52]The labeling in figure one is incomplete. Compare figure two.

[53]To complete the operation, the line is then tied off at the cleat on the support post.

[52]French, *ferme*. A *ferme* can be any type of frame which is covered with cloth, although in this discussion Boullet is referring specifically to ground rows which are carried to the stage by the cassettes.

[53]A sloat is a very narrow trap running the entire width of the stage to allow passage for flat scenery carried by the cassettes.

[54]The Paris *toise* was equivalent to approximately six feet.

[55]French, *traverse*. This term refers to any horizontal member used in flat construction and means both "rail" and "toggle."

[56]This is not true as a generality. This statement only applies to heavy grid machinery or to machines with special requirements, such as the act curtain.

[57]Label *G* is missing from the drawing.

[58]This is the regulator at the drum. There are two regulators used on this machine, one at the drum and another attached to the counterweight.

[59]*Livres* is assumed.

[60]Boullet is playing on words since "Théâtre des Arts" not only means "Art Theatre" but it is also the name of the theatre which housed the Paris Opera when he wrote this book.

[61]Labels are missing from this plate.

[62]Boullet's original text is confusing here since he reverses the actual order of routing the rigging. A literal translation of his text would read: "Having attached one end of these lines to a drum as for a glory which is supposed to move up and down, the other ends are passed through the two sheaves at either end of the trolley *D* and then around the two sheaves which are in a block *V*, located above the place where the car is supposed to arrive."

[63]Giovanni Nicolo Servandoni, 1695-1766.

[64]That is, prevent fire from spreading from the grid to the attic over the auditorium or *vice versa*.

[65]The *muid* of Paris was equal to 268 liters or 74.44 gallons.

[66]French, *convenablement élastique*.

[67]Carlo Fontana, 1634-1714, was a famous Italian architect, known mainly for his work on churches and other public buildings, but his great contribution to Theatre was the Teatro Tor di Nona which he built in Rome in 1671.

[68]Henri Louis Lekain, 1729-1778, also known as Kain, was a famous actor on the Paris stage.

[69]French, *peintre-decorateur*.

[70]French, *decorateur*.

[71]1796.

[72]French, *planter une ouvrage.*

[73]French, *sauter des plans.*

[74]Boullet is referring to a street in the set, not a division of the stage.

[75]Here, "perspective" probably refers to a painted dropcloth, not perspective on the stage since the term had been commonly used in this sense since the seventeenth century. The ambiguity in this translation remains just as it is in Boullet's text.

[76]Since all the wings stood parallel to each other, facing the audience, a performer could enter between any two of them regardless of what they may have depicted. Consequently, one could literally enter through a wall.

[77]French, *peintre-decorateur.*

[78]French, *peintre.*

[79]French, *decorateur.*